MW00978462

A Writer's Handbook

A Writer's Handbook

Developing Writing Skills for University Students

fourth edition

**Edited by
Leslie E. Casson**

broadview press

BROADVIEW PRESS – www.broadviewpress.com
Peterborough, Ontario, Canada

Founded in 1985, Broadview Press remains a wholly independent publishing house. Broadview's focus is on academic publishing; our titles are accessible to university and college students as well as scholars and general readers. With over 600 titles in print, Broadview has become a leading international publisher in the humanities, with world-wide distribution. Broadview is committed to environmentally responsible publishing and fair business practices.

The interior of this book is
printed on 100% recycled paper.

© 2018 Leslie E. Casson

All rights reserved. No part of this book may be reproduced, kept in an information storage and retrieval system, or transmitted in any form or by any means, electronic or mechanical, including photocopying, recording, or otherwise, except as expressly permitted by the applicable copyright laws or through written permission from the publisher.

Library and Archives Canada Cataloguing in Publication

Writer's handbook (Kingston, Ont.)
    A writer's handbook : developing writing skills for university students
/ edited by Leslie E. Casson. — Fourth edition.

Includes bibliographical references.
ISBN 978-1-55481-370-4 (softcover)

    1. English language—Rhetoric—Handbooks, manuals, etc. 2. English language—Grammar—Handbooks, manuals, etc. 3. Report writing—Handbooks, manuals, etc. I. Casson, Leslie Elizabeth, 1966-, editor
II. Queen's University (Kingston, Ont.). Writing Centre, issuing body
III. Title.

PE1478.W75 2018   808'.042   C2017-907757-0

Broadview Press handles its own distribution in North America:
PO Box 1243, Peterborough, Ontario K9J 7H5, Canada
555 Riverwalk Parkway, Tonawanda, NY 14150, USA
Tel: (705) 743-8990; Fax: (705) 743-8353
email: customerservice@broadviewpress.com

Distribution is handled by Eurospan Group in the UK, Europe, Central Asia, Middle East, Africa, India, Southeast Asia, Central America, South America, and the Caribbean. Distribution is handled by Footprint Books in Australia and New Zealand.

Broadview Press acknowledges the financial support of the Government of Canada through the Canada Book Fund for our publishing activities.

Copy-edited by Martin R. Boyne
Interior design and typeset by Eileen Eckert
Cover design by Em-Dash Design

PRINTED IN CANADA

Contents

Acknowledgements

This small book is a collaborative effort, the cumulative wisdom of colleagues past and present at the Writing Centre at Queen's University. I am grateful for their expertise, their time and effort, and their generosity. Editing this book has been like sitting in on tutorials with some of the most experienced, most gifted writing teachers one could ever hope to find, and I am a better teacher and a more disciplined writer for it. Thanks also to our students, for engaging and challenging us, and to Marjorie Mather, Martin Boyne, and the folks at Broadview, for their continued support.

Of course, guiding it all from the beginning was Dr. Doug Babington, contributor, mentor, advocate, colleague, and friend. As Director of the Queen's Writing Centre, he always delighted in the particular and peculiar gifts of his staff and drew from us our best efforts. This book provides a snapshot of the kind of work he fostered and grew at Queen's. On behalf of us all: Doug, thank you.

contributors

Doug Babington

Kevin Brushett

Les Casson

Shannon Chace-Hall

Maureen Garvie

Grant Heckman

Susan Korba

Darragh Languay

Christian Lloyd

Rosalind Malcolm

Stephanie Novak

Susan Olding

Shannon Smyrl

Irwin Streight

one Understanding the Assignment

When many students think about essays, they focus on the end product: *Will it be long enough? Will it be finished on time?* And, of course, *How much sleep will I lose getting there?* Although this section won't guarantee a full night's rest, a few comments on how to begin an essay may help pilot the process of completing one.

An undergraduate essay is more than a 12-page paper; it is an exercise in thinking, organizing, and writing. The first step in producing a successful paper is fully understanding the assignment. More than a general hunch, this understanding must be precise and focused. Sometimes, students end up writing essays that stray from the matter at hand, answering questions related to, but other than, the ones posed by the assignment. Always discuss and clear variations on the topic with your professor or marker; that way, you can get full credit for your efforts. A well-written essay that veers off topic cannot receive the grade the writing itself merits.

looking for action

When you first receive your assignment, look closely at the actions described in the topic or question—the verbs. In the same way that the given assignment topic helps define *what* you are to do (the scope of the paper), the verbs in the question give clues as to *how* to approach your essay. Look for words such as *analyze, evaluate, compare, contrast, discuss, assess, describe,* or *review*. Also, keep an eye out for nouns that imply action (such as *analysis, evaluation, comparison, assessment,* etc.). If the assignment contains more than one of these action words, think about how you might use them to organize your paper; they might provide natural subdivisions in the essay's structure. Be sure to distinguish key points of focus in the assignment from supplementary ones and give appropriate weight to these central ideas in your paper.

Here is a sample topic:

William Blake and William Wordsworth are central figures of the Romantic Movement. Through a textual analysis of their poetry and by situating the authors in their historical context, discuss the central tenets of Romanticism. Your essay must also consider the relationship between Enlightenment ideals and the Romantic Movement.

The main task of the assignment is to "*discuss* the central tenets of Romanticism." The assignment also specifies how the student is expected to go about this task: by analyzing the two authors' poetry and by situating the writers in their historical context. Thus, by looking at the poetry and the historical situation in which it was written, the student writer should be able to make some observations about Romanticism itself. In other words, look at Romanticism through the given lens (i.e., the poetry and the historical conditions of the poets) and tell your reader what you see. These observations will provide the main focus for your discussion.

Finally, the assignment asks you to consider the relationship between Enlightenment ideals and the Romantic Movement. This requirement is introduced by the phrase "your essay must also," which suggests that this sub-topic is not the paper's central focus. Thus you will need to say something about this relationship, but these points will supplement or reflect on your main discussion of Romanticism rather than form the central focus of your paper.

The following chart defines some of the terms most frequently used in writing assignments:

ANALYZE (OUTLINE/ EXPLAIN)	separate the matter at hand into key parts, essential elements; break things down, consider the details; identify causes, key factors or features, possible results.
COMPARE	note similarities and differences between two or more things.
CONTRAST	note differences, dissimilarities, tensions between two or more things.
EXAMINE (EXPLORE/ INVESTIGATE)	take a diagnostic approach; inquire or look into closely, perhaps to uncover a hidden motive, theme, etc.; seek out core issues, suggest possible interpretations or solutions.
ARGUE	take a position on a given subject and support that approach; give reasons for or against something.
DEBATE	present opposing viewpoints on a given subject; deliberate; give reasons for and against something.
EVALUATE (JUDGE/ CRITICIZE/ INVESTIGATE)	determine the value or significance of something.
DESCRIBE	depict, present, or delineate in words; place more emphasis on how something occurs than on why.
DEFINE	give the meaning of something; present its nature or essential qualities.
TRACE	follow the course, development, or history of something.

REVIEW	summarize the key aspects of the material at hand.
DOCUMENT	like "TRACE," follow the development, course, or history of something, but emphasize the use of written sources, references, and citations in supporting your approach; prove using written support material, concrete sources, and evidence.
DISCUSS	comment on, talk over, write about the topic at hand using whatever approach seems appropriate (i.e., any of the approaches listed in this chart).

different verbs, different essays

The action words used in an assignment also tell you what kind of essay you are to produce. Verbs such as *evaluate, assess,* or *analyze* announce that your essay will be argumentative, requiring a clearly stated thesis or central argument. (This approach is also true of assignments that present a statement or assertion and then say "Discuss.") If the central verb in the assignment is *outline* or *describe*, then the essay should clearly present the pertinent information on a given subject, rather than argue or defend a particular approach to that subject. If you are asked to *compare and contrast*, then the assignment requires you to discuss the two (or more) issues, positions, or texts at hand in relation to each other, isolating the principal ways in which they are fundamentally alike and/or different.

A critical book review assumes a slightly different approach than a standard essay. Rather than write on the same topic as the book in question, you are required to critique the book's approach to that topic (i.e., *review* the author's efforts). To do so, you must first summarize and characterize the book's primary contents (thesis, approach, research, etc.) and then offer an assessment of the strengths and weaknesses of that author's project. A book review of Thomas Cahill's *How the Irish Saved Civilization*, then, would not be an essay about Irish history but an essay discussing and evaluating Cahill's approach to the subject in his book.

For the most part, an assignment topic defines the general scope of your essay. It points you in a particular direction and asks you to go exploring. The action words in the assignment topic give further instruction on how to approach your writing project and on what kinds of information to bring back from your travels. So look to the verbs and look for the action. Take time to determine the exact nature of the task at hand (i.e., what you are being asked to do) and then stay focused on that task. Beginning the writing process with a clear sense of what is expected of you will help you to further define your particular approach to the assignment.

two Planning and Outlining

Once you have come to a solid understanding of the topic, you need to begin defining the focus and shape of your essay. Through careful planning and outlining, you can better determine the purpose and approach of your paper—what you want to do and how you wish to do it—before launching into your first draft.

This phase of the writing process is often given short shrift. Students often feel as if they are not accomplishing anything at this point, but instead are spending an incredible amount of time with no tangible results. Frankly, the planning stage is the most time-consuming part of the writing process; it involves a great deal of reading, scribbling, mulling, and backtracking. And then more scribbling. And more mulling. However, this stage is crucial to creating a successful paper. Time spent considering your own ideas, exploring new approaches, following hunches, and comparing observations will lead to a more thoughtful, substantial (and therefore persuasive) piece of writing in the end. So take heart and dig in!

gathering material

The first thing to do at this stage is to begin gathering your own thoughts. There are a number of ways you can do this, depending on your own learning style. Here are some suggestions:

- Create folders on your device for each project, saving them to your desktop or in the cloud or a shared document so they are readily available. As you assemble materials from your research and drafting, keep track of them in the relevant folder.

- Keep a running log of your ideas in a document and save this to your folder as well. Depending on how developed this log gets, it may provide useful fodder for an outline.

- Try brainstorming or freewriting before you hit the library or the web. Write your topic at the top of the page, set a timer for 2–3 minutes, and start typing. Write down everything that comes to mind in relation to that topic. Don't edit or pause to consider your work until the timer is finished. (If you're working at a desktop computer, try turning off the monitor while you write.) Once finished, review what you've written, highlighting any key words, phrases, or notions that strike you as promising. This exercise can take a little getting used to, but with practice it can become a valuable tool for clearing your mind and for discovering what you already know or think about a topic.

- Speaking of brainstorming, take time to experiment with a few productivity, whiteboard, or note-taking apps in the early weeks of term—before essay panic sets in. Used deliberately, these can help you organize and track your thinking and can end up being great time-savers when your workload gets heavier.

- When researching sources online, remember to keep track of when and where you found the material. In addition to recording standard details such as title, author, etc., keep a record of the URL, the date the page was last revised, and the date on which you accessed the information. You'll need these details when it comes time to document your sources. In fact, recording all bibliographic information carefully as you conduct your research can save you time and headaches later.

- If you're someone who tends to think out loud, use your device's camera or microphone as a way of making notes. Take a few minutes to talk through your ideas and then review the sound/video file as you would the freewriting/brainstorming above. You may even want to consider software (such as Dragon®) that transforms speech into text in your word-processing program.

- Sometimes, moving from electronic to hard-copy tools (and vice versa) can slow down or speed up your brainstorming, either of which can be helpful in generating ideas. Don't be afraid to mix your media. If you find yourself hitting a brick wall with your usual strategy, try changing it up. Any of the above strategies can work using physical tools (pen and paper, cue cards, a whiteboard, sticky notes, etc.), and often having something concrete to work with can help you stay focused. Once you're finished with the hands-on tools, take a picture of your work and upload it to your project folder. That way, you'll always have access to your materials and a record of your thought process.

When it comes to gathering your ideas, there are no right or wrong methods. The only rule is to do it—keep track of your thoughts. By not keeping a record, you may forget ideas, misplace quotations and documentation info, or lose track of insights or creative touches that could become central points later on. Furthermore, maintaining a tangible record of your thoughts may help you get some sleep when your mental filing cabinet is over-full; when it is time for a break, files can be saved and set aside more easily than can an over-worked brain scrambling to remember details.

what/how/why

Having taken the time to brainstorm your initial ideas, now sit down at your keyboard or arm yourself with the necessary pens, cards, or crayons and re-read your primary materials with an eye to the essay topic. As you read, ask yourself questions about content and form— *what* is said and *how* it is said. If a passage leaps out to you, mark it so that you can go back and examine it more closely. Ask yourself *why* this passage seems significant. *Keep asking why* until you come up with a satisfactory response; press your analysis. The more you can articulate for yourself *why* something matters, the more you will be able to explain your thoughts in the essay.

As you gather your observations, look for relationships between ideas—patterns, contrasts, etc.—and start classifying your notes under different headings. These headings will vary from paper to paper. For example, in the case of a film or literature paper, you may begin with categories such as

character   conflict   genre   imagery   plot

and make notes from there. If your paper seeks to examine an historical or sociological phenomenon, you might break it down into

| social impacts | economic impacts | psychological impacts | political impacts. |

Another approach might be to use key words from the assignment question—verbs, major concepts—as initial categories and then further narrow your focus from there. Regardless of where you begin, your categories should become more refined as you compile information and observe relationships between concepts. Gradually, you will begin to build a framework for your ideas—a framework that may provide the internal structure for your paper.

For those papers requiring secondary sources (criticism, biographies, journal articles), hold off on consulting them until you have a good grasp of the primary material, lest your own insights be overshadowed by someone else's observations. It is easy to inadvertently absorb someone else's perspective or turn-of-phrase into your own opinion. Keep careful track of what you glean from secondary readings; doing so will help you avoid plagiarism. Also, avoid becoming overly reliant on secondary material. Outside sources should serve as springboards, catalysts, or supports for your own analysis; they should not replace your own thinking on the topic. When you do turn to secondary sources, read them while actively questioning how they fit with your own interpretations and opinions. Again, consider *what* is being said, *how* it is said, and *why* that point may be significant to the overall project. It should be clear, in your writing, that you have thought critically about your secondary sources, that you understand the background and implications of what you have read, and that you are able to apply these theories and ideas in new contexts. Quotations should be used only when they are particularly pointed or well expressed and work to serve your argument.

organizing material—developing your thesis and outline

Once you have spent time exploring the material in question and organizing your observations, start developing the thesis—the central argument—of your paper. Sometimes students confuse their *topic* with their *thesis*. The assignment topic outlines the general scope of your project; the thesis focuses your discussion of that topic. A thesis is a statement that takes a position or offers an interpretation of the subject at hand; it is not simply a description or a statement of fact.

Consider the following example. The course is "The Sociology of Religion in North America" and the assignment topic is as follows:

> Researchers have noted that while attendance at mainstream Christian churches has declined in the last quarter century, interest in Evangelical Christianity has increased. By considering social factors such as race, age, class, or gender, suggest reasons for this shift.

In this case, the student begins her research with the information outlined in the topic:

> While attendance at mainstream Christian churches has declined in the last quarter century, interest in Evangelical Christianity has increased.

Then she begins to ask herself, "*Why is this the case?*" As she continues her research, the student discovers that these churches have done a lot of new things to appeal to people. They have changed the shape of their buildings, adding gyms and daycare facilities, etc. They have also changed the look and feel of a Sunday-morning service, forgoing traditional organ music and hymns for pop-styled songs with full band accompaniment. She also notices that a lot of the big churches sell recordings, videos, and books, and most are active on social media. As she thinks about her findings, she develops a new working thesis:

> By appealing to contemporary consumer appetites, Evangelical Christian churches have repackaged their faith and, as a result, increased their numbers.

With that new working thesis in hand, she tries to push her ideas further, using the *what/how/why* strategy mentioned above. This approach helps her move from a descriptive position to an interpretive one.

WHAT	Evangelical Christians have increased numbers by appealing to consumer appetites
HOW	1. changes in buildings and programs: multi-purpose buildings, lifestyle programming 2. changes in Sunday-morning worship style: bands, visuals, computer slideshows 3. portability: material goods, books, recordings, videos, podcasts, social media 4. demographics: the churches seem to appeal to young families, affluent people, etc.
WHY	These changes reflect middle-class, suburban values; numbers are up, but those who aren't middle class don't seem to fit.

As she works through her observations, the student realizes that she could consider class factors in her argument. According to her research, a lot of the people going to these churches are young professionals with families. Multi-purpose buildings appeal to their needs, as do the portable resources. She realizes that she could not only make a case for who is being drawn into these churches and why, but also suggest reasons why certain groups might be left out. Having spent time looking into the implications of her observations—*why* her observations might be significant—she is able to come up with a more sophisticated thesis:

> By appealing to consumer appetites, Evangelical churches have repackaged their faith in a way that reflects and promotes middle-class, suburban values. While this shift has helped to increase numbers, it has also excluded those who fall outside these implicit social and economic parameters.

By taking the time to consider *why* the observations matter, the writer has deepened the discussion. The thesis not only makes detailed observations about the source material, but it also suggests a way to interpret this material. From this point, the essay becomes a matter of supporting and developing that interpretation.

When you use a *what/how/why* breakdown, the heart of the thesis usually rests in the *why* statement. A thesis that addresses only *what* and *how* usually ends up being merely descriptive. The *why* component foregrounds your interpretation of the data presented, which is the core of your paper. What your reader is most interested in is your take on the information—your interpretation or approach to the matter at hand—not just a summary of the details involved. A thesis statement that answers *what/how/why* in one to two sentences gives your paper a precise focus. It shows your reader that you know where you're going and why it is worthwhile to get there.

Once you have developed a satisfactory working thesis, start shaping an outline for your paper. This process will give you a sense of the big picture and help you to stay focused as you write. An outline is a chart, a road map, or a thumbnail-sketch of your paper. It lays out key ideas, the order in which they will be developed, and some provisional conclusions (sometimes the *what/how/why* strategy can help you frame your points at this stage, too). It is important to remember, however, that an outline is simply a guide. Arguments always change somewhat in the writing; by developing your points more fully, you will begin to discover what your ideas really are and where they can take you. Therefore, your thesis does not need to be set in stone at this point, but it does need some definite shape. Taking the time to develop a clear working thesis and outline enables you to approach the first draft—and any new ideas that strike you as you write—with greater confidence. As you begin to draft your essay, stay focused but stay flexible, too. Try to keep a balance between maintaining your initial direction and staying open to new ideas that may emerge as you write.

three **Paragraphs**

Once you have spent some time drafting your ideas and honing your thesis and outline in response to this first draft, it is time to work on shaping your expression paragraph by paragraph. Your thesis articulates the purpose and trajectory of the paper; well-focused paragraphs carry the reader through the logic of that argument. Essentially, paragraphs break the argument down into manageable pieces, highlighting your key ideas and the relationships among them. A paragraph that is too short, too long, or lacking in coherent structure obscures your ideas, leaving the reader confused, bored, or baffled. An effective paragraph gives the reader sufficient information to grasp both the issue at hand and its significance within your overall argument.

the long and the short of it

Determining the best length for a paragraph should not be governed so much by the number of sentences it contains as by the function of those sentences. Any given paragraph should be as long as is needed to introduce and then analyze or describe the topic at hand. Very short paragraphs—those that are one to four sentences in length—usually lack the scope to develop an idea fully. They give the reader too brief a glimpse of the matter in question, often leaving one of two impressions: either the point is not really worth discussing, or the writer does not really understand it in the first place. On the other hand, overly long paragraphs try to do too many things at once. Although they may contain good information and analysis, they too often lose focus, leaving the reader lost as well. It may be that your main point has been superseded by a follow-up idea (one that, perhaps, warrants its own paragraph) or that you have buried the point in too many similar examples. Perhaps you have simply said the same thing three different ways. No matter how good your information may be, it is of little use to your readers if they have to go mining for it. Both long and short paragraphs can be used effectively for specific stylistic or organizational ends, but for the purposes of most undergraduate essays, extremely short or long paragraphs should be avoided.

what/how/why ... again

When editing a paragraph for length, look at the functions of the sentences involved. *What* point are you trying to make, and *how* are you choosing to argue it? *Why* is the point significant in light of both previous ideas and the overall project itself? Applying the *what/how/why* strategy to paragraph structure may help you stay focused.

WHAT (the Point)	The main idea to be discussed (best introduced in a *topic sentence*, the introductory sentence to your paragraph)	1–2 sentences
HOW (the Support or Proof)	The evidence used to substantiate the point or back up the argument: examples, appropriate reference material, quotations, etc.	2–4 sentences
WHY (the Comment)	Commentary outlining the significance of the preceding material Your explanation of how and why these ideas fit together: relationships, contrasts, conclusions, etc.	2–4 sentences

Certainly, the above chart is intended as a guide, not a grid. Not every paragraph functions in the manner described above; however, the *what/how/why* strategy can serve as a helpful logic-barometer for your writing. For example, if it takes more than one or two sentences to introduce the point of the paragraph, it is likely that you are trying to focus on too much or that you are unclear about the precise focus. Having fewer than two sentences of supporting evidence or commentary usually signals a minor point; perhaps this idea is actually part of a larger notion rather than a discrete point requiring a paragraph of its own. Conversely, more than four sentences of commentary or supporting information might signal one of two things: you may be making the same point several times over (rather than *building* on a point with each sentence) or your evidence may be straying off into a new area, which should merit a separate paragraph.

focus and coherence

Effective paragraphs manage to focus on an idea and develop it. As you edit your draft, make sure that the sentences in your paragraph relate *directly* to not only the general topic of the essay but also the specific idea or argument expressed in the topic sentence. Just because a sentence relates to the topic in question does not necessarily make it relevant to the point you are arguing. Take the following example.

> Over the years, capital punishment has not significantly reduced violent crime. Statistics show that the number of murders in jurisdictions without capital punishment is no higher than in those jurisdictions that impose capital punishment for murder convictions. Interviews with those convicted of premeditated murder on death row have also revealed that the idea that they might die for

their actions never entered their minds prior to or during the murder. Moreover, these same statistics reveal it is more than twice as likely that convicted black murderers will receive the death penalty than their white counterparts. This is clearly an injustice that must be righted.

The above paragraph is successful until the end of the third sentence. The second and third sentences work to develop the main idea of the first sentence. The fourth and fifth sentences, however, are out of place in this paragraph. The fourth sentence still deals with capital punishment and violent crime so it is not completely off-topic. However, the main idea introduced in this sentence—that convicted blacks are more likely to be executed than whites—is largely irrelevant to the *particular* argument introduced in the first sentence (i.e., the relationship between capital punishment and the deterrence of violent crimes). The fifth sentence builds upon the previous sentence but switches the focus again toward the idea of injustice, which, although important, does not help prove the point that capital punishment does not deter violent crime. Although the content of the fourth and fifth sentences is generally related to issues of capital punishment, it does not relate to the particular focus of the paragraph. Instead of tacking it on to the end of this paragraph, take time to explore and develop it in a new one.

transitions

Not only do you need to show the relationships between the ideas within a paragraph, but you must also move naturally between major points in different paragraphs. This ability to make successful transitions between ideas contributes to the overall flow and coherence of your paper. When it comes to reinforcing the links between paragraphs, some methods include using a key word from the preceding paragraph, reminding the reader of your thesis, or beginning a paragraph with a sentence that refers to an idea developed in a previous paragraph.

For example, imagine you are writing a paper arguing that the presidency of John F. Kennedy was one of the most important in all of American history. You have just finished writing a paragraph discussing Kennedy's role in promoting the Apollo space program as a particularly important facet of American foreign policy. However, you want to shift the focus of the essay away from foreign-policy issues and toward domestic issues such as Kennedy's impact on the civil rights movement. How do you link these two very disparate topics? Here is one suggestion:

> While Kennedy challenged NASA to put an American on the moon by the end of the decade, his presidency faced challenges of its own from the civil rights movement.

Or you could try it this way:

> While Kennedy's promotion of the Apollo space program was an important part of United States foreign policy during his presidency, the civil rights movement proved to be the most important domestic issue facing him during his brief tenure in the Oval Office.

In both of these examples, the writer uses a particular concept to serve as a hinge joining the two topics—a *hook*. The first transition focuses on *challenges*, showing that Kennedy both issued and was faced by challenges during his presidency. The second pivots on *importance*, linking the space program and civil rights as similarly key issues despite their different spheres of foreign and domestic policy. Both are succinct and clever transitions.

In addition to such conceptual hooks, simple transitional words and phrases can aid the process of linking ideas within and between paragraphs. The chart below outlines some common transitional words, as well as their logical contexts.

ADDITION	CONSEQUENCE	DIVERSION	GENERALIZATION
also besides furthermore in addition moreover too what is more as well as	accordingly as a result consequently hence so then thus therefore	by the way incidentally	as a rule for the most part generally in general usually ordinarily
CONTRAST	**COMPARISON**	**SEQUENCE**	**RESTATEMENT**
however by contrast conversely instead on the other hand contrarily rather yet nevertheless even so otherwise	likewise in the same way in comparison comparatively speaking similarly	afterwards at the same time for now in time later on next then subsequently first, second, etc. at first finally first of all in turn to begin with	in essence in other words namely that is that is to say
ILLUSTRATION	**INTENSIFICATION**	**SUMMARY**	
for example for instance for one thing	indeed in fact simply stated simply put	in closing to sum up on the whole in brief	

Like any other tool, transitional words can be overused. Be sure of the shift you are making before you signal a transition to your reader. Sprinkling an awkward paragraph with a few choice transitional words and phrases will not compensate for woolly thinking or a poorly structured argument.

A final note on transitions: avoid ending paragraphs with a transitional sentence that introduces an entirely new point. Although some secondary school curricula advocate this strategy as an effective way of linking ideas, it becomes awkward and even gimmicky as essays become longer and more sophisticated. Often this transitional sentence is more effective as a topic sentence for the next paragraph. Structure your paragraph around a core idea; once that idea has been developed satisfactorily, move on to the next point in a new paragraph. It is better to link backwards (using a key word or phrase from the preceding paragraph as noted above) than to disrupt a completed argument by throwing in a yet-to-be related concept at the end.

beginnings and endings

As you edit your drafts for coherence and flow, keep an eye on the beginnings and endings of your paragraphs. Does the final sentence of the paragraph show a richer understanding of the concept introduced in the topic sentence? Does the topic sentence of the subsequent paragraph follow as a natural next step in the argument, either as a follow-up point or as an appropriately linked new idea? Sometimes this kind of editing strategy can help highlight the larger flow of your paper as it has developed over one or two drafts.

Furthermore, looking closely at the beginnings and endings of the paragraphs in your early drafts can help you shape the introductory and concluding paragraphs for your finished essay. Again, there are no hard and fast rules as to when to write your introduction and conclusion, but it is very common to save drafting those crucial paragraphs until you have completed the body of your essay. That way, you know more clearly what it is you are about to introduce and conclude. The beginnings and endings of your body paragraphs (i.e., the paragraphs that make up the bulk of your argument/ discussion) can give you clues as to what to include in these components. For example, look to the ends of these paragraphs (your *why* statements or commentary) when you begin writing your conclusion. As you look at the small conclusions you have drawn along the way, try to draw some larger conclusions about your paper as a whole. Again, consider *what* you have said, *how* those ideas might interact, and *why* those interactions are significant. Look at the relationships among the ideas—contrasts, tensions, etc.—and how those ideas relate to your thesis. Articulating these relationships and their significance can provide the heart of a successful conclusion.

Similarly, use the topic sentences of your body paragraphs to help shape your introduction. They introduce the ideas you wish to discuss; as such, these concepts, or some kind of summary of them, should be included in your introduction. So look at your topic sentences, make a list of the concepts, and then work on how best to articulate this content in your introduction. You may not need to list all of the concepts individually, particularly if some are related (different types of imagery in a literature essay, for example, could just be summarized as "imagery," especially if the essay deals with other major literary issues such as form, character, etc.). An effective introductory paragraph outlines the information the reader needs in order to make sense of the thesis statement. It should introduce key concepts, figures, themes, and/or principles and give some indication of how they will be examined in the paper. Introductions are like road maps—they tell the reader where you are going to take them and how they will get there. They also give some sense of why the journey is important. Also, avoid starting your introduction with "since the beginning of time" statements or other such sweeping pronouncements; they are a dead give-away that the writer does not know quite where to begin.

Instead, look for the key words in your assignment question to help you define the boundaries of the discussion. Generally speaking, for most undergraduate essays, a single, well-conceived paragraph that sets the parameters of the discussion and ends with the thesis statement will provide all the introduction you need.

know your project

When planning, drafting, and re-drafting your paper, remember that your job is not simply to lay out information but to show *how* this information works to create and sustain a point. Frankly, a well-crafted essay does not tell the reader everything the writer knows about a certain subject; instead, it articulates those things the writer feels the reader *must* understand in order to fully grasp a particular aspect of that subject. Thus the sentences in a given paragraph should work together to show relationships among the ideas, actions, or events described therein. Your job as a writer is to identify and explore the significance of these links and tensions for your reader. If you do not know why a point should be included, don't include it! Or better yet, figure out *why* it matters and tell your reader *that*. The more clearly and succinctly you can articulate the *what*s, *how*s, and *why*s of your paper, the more convincing that paper will be.

four Stylistic Decisions

In academic writing—or any kind of writing, for that matter—try to get the most mileage out of your ideas. In other words, good ideas deserve good expression. If your readers have to struggle just to get the meaning of a given sentence, they may well struggle with your overall argument, too. Far too often, good thinking gets lost in lumpy, weak, or awkward writing. Here are a few tips for sharpening your expression.

editing with your ears

One of the best ways to understand the rhythm of your writing is to listen to it. When editing your work, try reading it aloud. Slowly. If you only read your work silently, you can easily miss some writing errors or awkward turns of phrase by moving too quickly through the text. Particularly after you've been working on the piece for a long time, reading silently can numb you to what is actually on the page. You can easily start mentally filling in any blanks in logic, clarity, or phrasing, leaving what you actually say on the page very different than what you think you are saying. The ear picks up errors the eye misses.

Also, editing with your ears can help detect problems with phrasing and rhythm: monotonous phrasing (too many short sentences or too many long ones), unnecessary repetition (every sentence in the paragraph starts with "In the novel" or "The experiment"), sentence fragments, etc. This kind of editing can also help you *hear* your own writing style. It will help you notice if you structure all your sentences the same way (subordinate clause + independent clause, for example) and help you work to vary the rhythm of your expression. Try to mix it up a bit. Punctuate a dense paragraph of longer sentences and complex ideas with one or two short, sharp sentences. Nail the point. Becoming sensitive to the inherent rhythms of your writing will help you express your ideas with more confidence and force.

One way to develop your editorial ear is to respond to texts that you find easy or difficult to read. When you come across a paragraph that seems particularly lucid, take a few moments to read it closely. Try to work out how the pattern of stresses in each sentence and the varieties in sentence structure and length all help the reader progress through the text. Note how the author adjusts rhythm to emphasize key ideas. Look for patterns or models that you might incorporate into your own writing. Similarly, work your way through a passage that you find difficult to read. What are the patterns or stresses that impede your movement through the text? Look for ways in which a failure to consider rhythm obscures key ideas or draws attention to less important elements in a sentence or paragraph. Keep an eye out—or an ear open—for similar problems in your own writing.

content vs. grammar

In a way, sentences operate on two levels: one deals with content, the other with grammar. On the one hand, there is the idea you wish to express, the point you want to make, the story you are telling. That is the content. On the other, is the way you choose to express that idea—the words you use and their particular function in the sentence (as objects, modifiers, etc.). In a very simple way, that is the grammar. Often, if a sentence is poorly written, there is too large a gap between the content and the grammar. The content wants to express one idea, but the grammar expresses another. If you can close this gap and make the content do the grammatical work (say, of functioning as the core subject and verb), your sentence will express the idea more precisely. Take, for example, the following sentences from an essay on Robert Browning's poem "Porphyria's Lover."

The first is a relatively simple fix:

> It is by placing the psychological incident within the temporal bounds of a dramatic situation that Browning is able to compel readers to come to terms with the bizarre and irrational aspects of human nature.

Here, the main idea is easily clarified by removing the "it is ... that" construction:

> By placing the psychological incident within the temporal bounds of a dramatic situation, Browning is able to compel readers to come to terms with the bizarre and irrational aspects of human nature.

Shifting the focus from "it is ... that" to "Browning is able" sharpens the sentence. It puts the emphasis back on Browning and what he manages to accomplish in the poem. An even better edit would also tighten up the core verb, changing "is able to compel" to the simpler and stronger "compels":

> By placing the psychological incident within the temporal bounds of a dramatic situation, Browning compels readers to come to terms with the bizarre and irrational aspects of human nature.

Sometimes, however, *it is … that* sentences need more extensive editing to clarify their point. Consider the following sentence from the same essay:

It is this psychological development within the character of the speaker that Browning concentrates on throughout the course of the monologue.

As in the previous example, the grammatical core of this sentence (i.e., the subject and verb on which the rest of the sentence is built) is "it is." In terms of sentence structure, every other word refers back to this core in some way or another. The phrase "this psychological development" functions as the grammatical object of "it is." (The phrase answers the question "it is what?" It is "this psychological development.") The rest of the content follows this relatively simple subject-verb-object construction by way of two rather awkward prepositional phrases ("within the character" and "of the speaker"); a relative clause ("that Browning concentrates on"); and another pair of related prepositional phrases ("throughout the course" and "of the monologue"). The ideas of the sentence are buried in weak, subordinate constructions that depend, grammatically, on the words "it is." The result is a vague, convoluted sentence. The gap between the content and the grammar has weakened the writer's point, which has to do with the significance of Browning's concentration on his character's psychological development. In contrast, a more efficient sentence might be built around this core idea. In other words, make "Browning" the subject and work from there:

> Throughout the monologue, Browning concentrates on his speaker's psychological development.

By focusing on the *idea* and allowing that core idea to function also as the *grammatical* core of the sentence, the writer has not only clarified her point but sharpened her expression as well. What was confusing in twenty-one words is now much clearer in ten.

Generally speaking, avoid overusing *it is ... that* constructions (or *the fact of the matter is that* and other such "*that*-isms"). Such set-up phrases work well when the point requires particular formality or emphasis, as in the case of scientific prose; however, when used indiscriminately, they quickly bog down your writing, camouflaging the core ideas. Always try to express yourself as directly and actively as possible. Eliminating the verbal underbrush will help sharpen your expression.

to be or not ...

Along these same lines, beware of overusing the verb *to be* (*is*, *was*, *are*). Since *to be* expresses a state of being rather than a clear action, overusing it can make your ideas seem vague. Often sentences that use a form of *to be* as a core verb have another, clearer action word buried somewhere else in the sentence; these words are expressed as simple verbs or cunningly disguised as nouns (*decision* instead of *decides*, for example) and describe, in many cases, the implicit action of the sentence. Here's an example:

> It is Woolf 's juxtaposition between being an inheritor of a civilization on the one hand and critical of it on the other that makes her a prime example of DuPlessis's "divided consciousness."

This sentence provides several examples of disguised verbs: juxtaposition/juxtapose; example/exemplify; being an inheritor/inherit. In this case, the writer decided to work with juxtapose and follow up with exemplify to refocus his sentence. This editing strategy made for a clearer and stronger statement:

> Woolf's text juxtaposes her roles of inheritor and critic of civilization; the resulting tension exemplifies what DuPlessis calls "divided consciousness."

Generally, if you come across a particularly ornery sentence—one that is really vague or convoluted—but cannot figure out how to better express the idea, try breaking your sentence down to its core components. Again, ask yourself *who's doing what?* and isolate the core *subject* and *verb*, the backbone of your sentence. Dissecting a sentence in this manner can help you better understand where the problem lies—whether it is in what you want to say or in how you have chosen to say it.

prepositional phrases

Another factor that can often slow down the rhythm of your sentences is overuse of prepositional phrases, particularly those beginning with *of*. Prepositions are words that indicate place or context: *of, over, around, under, in*, etc. Prepositional phrases begin with a preposition and tend to be two to four words in length: *in* the garden, *of* the novel, *under* the ugly couch, etc. Since these kinds of phrases generally contain only one piece of information, it is deceptively easy to string several of them together in a sentence, thereby bogging down the rhythm:

In the novels **of** Margaret Atwood, female protagonists **with** complex emotional problems tend to narrate **in** the first person leaving the reader **with** an unstable sense **of** the true story.

The point of editing this sentence is not to eliminate all the prepositional phrases but to streamline the expression so as to emphasize the most important ideas. In this case, the writer wants to highlight the tension between the reader and the narrator in Atwood's novels rather than the narrator's gender (an observation that can be developed later).

In Atwood's novels, the first-person narrator's emotional complexity tends to destabilize the reader's view **of** the story.

The sentence has gone from six prepositional phrases to two, but the wording is still a bit awkward. The question at this point is still *what information is crucial at this stage of the discussion?* Is it that the narrator is a first-person narrator or that the narrator is emotionally complex? By isolating the key information, you can better craft not only this sentence but also the sentences that follow.

> In Atwood's novels, the narrator's emotional complexity tends to destabilize the reader. By using a first-person narrator with a flawed perspective, Atwood forces her readers to interpret rather than simply accept the narrator's point of view and, in so doing, to assemble the story for themselves.

By working to isolate and focus on the key idea in the sentence, the writer has clarified her expression. Not only are there fewer prepositional phrases (the initial problem), but, through the revision process, several vague concepts ("true story," for example) have been further clarified. The result is a clearer, more thorough comment and a more focused start to her paragraph.

tone

Just as social situations require differing tones of voice and behaviour (football games vs. funerals, for example), writing assignments assume particular tones of voice and expression depending on their purpose and intended audience. Often students make the mistake of adopting either an artificial or stilted tone of expression in an academic paper or an overly casual one. For most academic writing, a direct, professional approach is appropriate. Imagine your audience to be not only the professor and teaching assistants but also the other students in the class, or an audience of similarly informed individuals. In other words, maintain a straightforward and natural tone of voice, one that seriously engages the course material without straining to sound intellectual. Avoid using contractions (*won't* for will not, *it's* for it is, etc.). Also, try to avoid speaking in the first person (I think, we believe, etc.), unless the assignment explicitly invites that approach. In some ways, a well-written paper sounds a bit like a polished version of the writer's own speaking voice; the expression is simply more organized and disciplined than it might be in regular conversation.

Finally, be careful to avoid using text-message syntax. While WTFYRUL8? might be a meaningful message to send to a friend who's forgotten to pick you up, no form of text-speak is appropriate in a professional or academic document. Steer clear of texting shortcuts: capitalize *I* when speaking of yourself, use *you* instead of *u*, and never, ever LOL.

beware your thesaurus

Careful word choice (often called "diction" in writing guides) is fundamental to effective writing. The most important thing to remember on this front is to use the right word (or words) for the job. A thesaurus is a dangerous weapon in the hands of someone desperate for synonyms; searches under duress often result in weirdly inflated language or just plain bafflegab. To avoid repeated errors and increase your vocabulary, make a habit of looking up familiar or semi-familiar words in a good dictionary, either print or online. A good dictionary will also provide information on nuances of usage, which will help you apply new vocabulary more effectively. Also, always cross-check in a dictionary the meaning of any term derived from a thesaurus. A dictionary is a far more precise tool than a thesaurus; make sure any noble quests for variety in word choice do not leave you lost in a forest of imprecision. It is very easy to retain a misleading notion of a word's exact meaning until the day you look it up.

figurative language

One often overlooked area of writing that can generate significant problems with tone is figurative language. Used well, it can clarify and enrich your argument; used poorly, it can confuse and distract your reader. Be careful when using similes, metaphors, and other figures of speech. Avoid clichés. An over-worn metaphor like "ballpark figure" (meaning "rough estimate") can deaden an interesting sentence. Conversely, outlandish similes can get you into trouble as well:

In Act II, Romeo burns with love for Juliet like a man who has just run out of Preparation H.

Here, the simile draws too much attention to itself. It distracts the reader from the idea by focusing too much on the way the idea is being expressed. When using figurative language, don't force it. Look for images that emerge intuitively from the context or that speak directly to the emotional focus of your idea. Even something as simple as

In Act II, Romeo's love for Juliet burns feverishly, deluding his judgement

is better than the drugstore simile above. At least here the writer can connect the fever image to Romeo's emotional state, comparing his infatuation with an overwhelming (and in his case, terminal) illness.

Generally speaking, use images that arise naturally from the context in question. Alternatively, if you want to use a contrasting image (i.e., one that is counterintuitive to the context), you must find a way to thread those contrasting or external images into the fabric of the piece. Even if they come as a surprise, the images must *feel* as if they belong there. The image must enhance or develop the idea; if it does not, it may well be an unnecessary extravagance.

Extravagant images are not the only common figurative errors to look out for, however. Mixed metaphors—figurative language that draws from two or more disparate images—always create tonal problems. Take for example, this metaphorical clunker:

> Mr. Murdoch was a viper who stabbed the workers in the back.

By mixing incomparable comparisons (knife-wielding snakes?), the sentence makes the idea being expressed seem implicitly ridiculous. Once again, a failure in the medium of figurative language has distorted the message. In the editing process, think carefully about the images you use. Make sure they paint a picture that enhances, rather than distracts from, your point.

be precise and be realistic

If you are stuck for a word to express a particular idea, or are uneasy about the one you have chosen, do not waste hours racking your mind over it. Sometimes there is no magic word to fill your needs. Try using a simple phrase to do the job. Also, remove (or substitute) words or phrases that will cause the average academic reader to have to reread the sentence.

Finally, make a list of words and phrases that instructors consistently mark in your term papers as inappropriate or vague, so that you can avoid using them. Examples of such taboo terms include *unique* and *obvious*. Is the item in question really unique in a particular way or is it simply unusual? If something is obvious, why are you discussing it? Do you really mean that the point is "evident" or "manifest"? And, unless you're being terribly clever with them, please avoid clichés. Even if you push the envelope 24/7, you'll never be able to drill down past this linguistic low-hanging fruit to curate the most amazeballs essay using clichés. Really.

five Essential Grammar

Nobody composes a first draft by pondering the "passive voice" or "pronoun case." When you begin to write, it is important to focus on your ideas and rely on your grammatical instincts. However, as you begin to hone and shape those ideas, the ability to analyze sentence structure—and to realize alternatives—is invaluable. The more familiar you become with essential grammar, the better and more confident you will be at revising your own work. The following principles will take you a long way.

clauses

Every clause contains a *subject* and a *verb*, which are also the key components of every sentence. The word *clause* is not, however, synonymous with the word *sentence*. Here's an example:

> If the level of corruption is extreme.

This clause does indeed contain a subject ("level") and a verb ("is"), but it is not a sentence—because it does not form a complete idea. Clauses that cannot stand as sentences are called dependent (or subordinate) clauses; they depend on stronger clauses for support:

> If the level of corruption is extreme, the mayor will face charges.

In this sentence, what follows the comma is known as an independent clause, since it contains a subject ("mayor") and a verb ("will face") and also forms a complete idea.

Successful writers keep a watchful eye on clauses: where they are placed, how they combine—and what exactly they contribute to the essay's clarity. Even a grammatically correct sentence can be a burden to read if its clauses are pushing and shoving at each other:

> If the level of corruption is extreme, the mayor, who has served with distinction over the past five years, exhibiting what many observers would call not only integrity but also imagination, will face charges that are serious, although no one expects that she will hesitate to emphasize that recent appointees be questioned vigorously concerning their involvement in the unfolding scandal.

The core of this unwieldy sentence is its independent clause: "the mayor will face charges." Unfortunately, the subject and verb are far apart, due to the intrusion of two dependent clauses (whose subject/verb combinations are "who has served" and "observers would call"). Still more dependent clauses trail after the independent clause (as with the others, you can locate them by pinpointing subject/verb combinations: "that are serious"; "although no one expects"; "that she will hesitate"; "that recent appointees be questioned"). Clauses are versatile and indispensable creatures. Their writers are responsible, though, for being able not only to recognize them but also to keep them under control.

voice: passive or active?

The interaction between subject and verb determines voice:

> The lawyers will present three scenarios.

> Three scenarios will be presented by the lawyers.

The first sentence features the active voice because its grammatical subject ("lawyers") performs the action represented by its verb ("will present"). By contrast, the second sentence features the passive voice; its grammatical subject ("scenarios") is acted upon by the verb ("will be presented").

Simply by counting words, you can see that the active voice is more concise than the passive voice (six words instead of eight). No doubt about it: the passive voice can lead to unnecessary wordiness. If, however, the fact that the lawyers are presenting the scenarios is understood, then the passive-voice version is not only clear but also concise:

Three scenarios will be presented.

Writers of laboratory reports often rely upon the passive voice for the same reason:

Thirteen replicates of the samples were examined.

Whenever the performer of an action is understood— or even unimportant or unknown—using the passive voice may well be appropriate. What matters most is your attentiveness as a writer. Casual reliance on the passive voice will certainly lead to flabby, overblown sentences:

Presentation of three scenarios will be undertaken by the lawyers.

Learning to write with a variety of sentence types is important, as it makes your writing more interesting and allows you to express more complex ideas. Connectors are words that join clauses, phrases, and words together in a sentence. There are four kinds of connectors: *coordinating conjunctions*, *correlative conjunctions*, *subordinating conjunctions*, and *conjunctive adverbs*.

Coordinating Conjunctions

Coordinating conjunctions join equal elements of a phrase or sentence. There are seven coordinating conjunctions: *and, but, or, nor, for, yet, so*.

> She didn't enjoy the concert, **yet** she bought a ticket for their next show.

> I love ice cream and kimchi, **but** not at the same time.

Correlative Conjunctions

Correlative conjunctions function much like coordinating conjunctions in that they also join equal elements; however, correlative conjunctions are always used in pairs: *both … and*; *not only … but also*; *either … or*; *neither … nor*.

> **Both** the model **and** the wrestler enjoyed rug hooking.

Subordinating Conjunctions

Subordinating conjunctions introduce dependent clauses, thereby indicating that what follows is *not* the main clause of the sentence. Some examples of subordinating conjunctions are *although, because, since, whenever, unless, in case.*

Since he didn't have a preference, I chose first.

She avoided the subway **because** it was overcrowded.

Conjunctive Adverbs

Conjunctive adverbs join independent clauses in a sentence (see also Chapter 6). Some examples are *afterward, consequently, however, nevertheless, therefore, thus.*

The storm destroyed the city; **consequently**, most people were left homeless.

she or her, who or whom? it all depends on the case

Nouns and pronouns function in sentences as either subjects or objects, and their appearance can change depending on their function. When a noun or pronoun is the subject of a sentence, it must be expressed in the subjective case. If it is an object, use the objective case.

When it comes to simple nouns, the changes in case forms are essentially invisible. The words switch position and function in the sentence, but the appearance of the actual words is left unchanged. For example, consider the following sentence:

The second demonstration halted traffic.

In this sentence, the noun "demonstration" is the subject, so it is expressed in the subjective case, and the noun "traffic" is the object, expressed in the objective case. Now, try switching their roles:

Traffic halted the second demonstration.

No big deal, right? The words are exactly the same. The only thing that changes is their grammatical function. So who cares? Pronouns care. Pronouns care a lot. When pronouns change case forms, their spelling changes as well:

They honked their horns at the demonstrators. ("They" is subjective)

Several demonstrators attacked them. ("them" is objective)

The perpetual question of "who or whom?" is a matter of pronoun case form. "Who" is the subjective case of the pronoun, and "whom" is the objective. If you're having trouble figuring out which one to use, try relating it to another pronoun:

Subjective	Objective
I	me
you	you
we	us
he/she/it	him/her/it
they	them
who/whoever	whom/whomever

For example, consider the following sentence.

> On reality shows, the producers can fire whomever/ whoever they choose.

If you are not sure whether to use who or whom, try rephrasing it. The part to focus on is "they choose...." Try to complete that part as a sentence on its own. If you were to complete the sentence using a different pronoun—such as he/him, for example—the sentence would read "they choose *him*," not "they choose *he*." This editing trick reveals that the pronoun is in the objective case (*him*, as opposed to the subjective *he*), so now you can write your original sentence with confidence:

On reality shows, the producers can fire whomever they choose.

Particularly tricky are phrases involving prepositions and pronouns (remember, prepositions are words that indicate place or context, such as *in*, *over*, *around*, *at*, *between*, and *from*). Each of the following examples is grammatically correct because the pronoun is functioning as the object of a preposition; therefore, the pronoun is written in its objective case form:

Talks between the company president and **him** were fruitful.

All of the memos from my supervisor and **me** will be archived.

As in the previous example, one way to check the pronoun is to rephrase the sentence. For instance, if the supervisor were not involved in the example above, the sentence would be simpler. Try substituting the pronoun *we*/*us*.

All of the emails from **us** will be archived.

One would write that the emails were "from us" rather than "from we." Therefore, the objective case form, *me*, is correct. Sometimes, mentally substituting the equivalent case form for another pronoun can help clarify which one to use in your sentence.

Another tricky situation involves pronouns used in dependent clauses:

A program will be distributed to whoever attends the performance.

Even though the pronoun "whoever" follows the preposition "to," it is written in the subjective case ("whoever" instead of "whomever") because it functions as the subject of a dependent clause ("whoever attends the performance"). The pronoun's function in a dependent clause always takes precedence.

Another important case—the possessive—causes one of the most common errors in academic writing: writing "it's" to mean "something belonging to it":

While watching the performance, we were impressed by it's lead actor.

This is wrong. The possessive form of the pronoun *it* must always be written *without* an apostrophe (i.e., *its*). Remember that *it's* can *only* be used as a contraction for the phrase *it is* or *it has*. If you find the word "it's" in an academic piece, review it carefully. It is either a spelling error for "its" or a tonal error, since you should avoid contractions in academic prose.

he, she, or they?: pronoun agreement and gender neutrality

Pronouns are the stunt-double of the grammatical world. Their job is to stand in for another noun in the sentence, freeing the writer (and reader) from annoying and wordy repetition. For example, rather than saying

> The President communicates from the President's Twitter account

we use the pronoun *he* to be more succinct:

> The President communicates from *his* Twitter account.

In setting up these relationships—between pronouns and their antecedents, the words they stand in for— writers must ensure that the words make sense together in terms of **number** (singular or plural), **person** (first, second, or third) and **gender** (masculine, feminine, or neutral). This is called pronoun agreement, and coming to that agreement is not always straightforward.

One point of confusion comes with indefinite pronouns, such as anyone, somebody, or nothing. These pronouns, ending with –one, –body, or –thing, are singular:

> *Somebody* left *his* or *her* pizza under the couch.

So why not keep it simple, and just use "their"? Good question. Technically, they/them/their are plural pronouns, so they clash with a singular antecedent. Historically, this clash was often remedied by defaulting to he/him/his:

> *Somebody* left *his* pizza under the couch.

However, this strategy creates sexist language. The argument that male pronouns can denote both male and female subjects has become antiquated, and this default use is no longer socially acceptable. For this reason, writers often rewrite the sentence as a plural statement, particularly when gender is not essential to the point. For example:

> *The party-crashers* left *their* pizza under the couch.

In this case, the focus of the sentence is less on the gender of the guests than it is their pizza-disposal behaviour, so the plural switch works.

But often gender is important to meaning, and the gender of the antecedent may not be clearly delineated by a simple *him* or *her*. On this, traditional English usage falls short. Unlike other languages, it lacks a neutral singular pronoun. In its place, forms of "they" are often used as a singular pronoun:

Somebody left *their* pizza under the couch.

This use is most common in casual speech, but is becoming more standard in written and academic English. Not only does the singular "they" keep indefinite pronouns neutral, but its use also recognizes that not everyone identifies along traditional gender binaries.

Taylor left *their* pizza under the couch.

Like many elements of language usage, this is an evolving practice. When choosing the singular "they," be mindful that some readers will still rankle at an apparent singular/plural clash. Know your audience, but also know your content. If your antecedent goes by "they," you should refer to them accordingly.

six Punctuation

Some writers punctuate by instinct, others by random guess. A secure knowledge of basic punctuation can free you up to write stronger, more sophisticated sentences. The following summary is intended to demystify some punctuation essentials. Consider it a user's guide.

that's all I have to say. period.

Periods indicate the end of a complete thought. However, when integrating quoted material into a sentence, place the sentence period *inside* the quotation marks and *outside* any parenthetical in-text citations.

> Hockey goalie Patrick Roy explains his success: "I talk to the goalposts."

> "Professional athletes do exciting, sometimes courageous, sometimes ennobling things, as heroes do, but no more than you do" (Dryden 376).

Periods are also used in abbreviations. They are uniformly used in familiar Latin abbreviations found in academic writing (et al., i.e., e.g., etc., ibid., viz., cf.). Generally, names of organizations that use acronyms do *not* take periods (NHL, GM, UAW, UN, NATO, WHO). Similarly, periods are unnecessary in the two-letter abbreviations of Canadian province and territory names (BC, MB, ON, NS, NU, etc.) and US state names (NY, CA, VT, GA, WY, etc.). Furthermore, there is a growing practice of dropping the periods in abbreviations of titles (Mrs, Mr, Dr, Col) and degrees (BA, MA, MBA, MSc, PhD). While this style of period-free abbreviation may save a few keystrokes, the trend is still new, and few usage guides recommend dropping the periods in standard abbreviations. It is also worth noting that neither "Ms" nor "Miss" is an actual abbreviation, so neither requires a period in the first place. Also, no period appears in the French abbreviations of Mademoiselle (Mlle) and Madame (Mme). Finally, Canadian writers tend to maintain the end periods in true abbreviations, such as manager (mgr.), assistant (asst.), Limited (Ltd.), and Saint (St.). American usage tends to drop these periods.

connecting ideas: commas and dashes

Generally speaking, *commas* link component parts of a sentence. While they often signal the natural pauses in the flow of a sentence, they are not breath marks; casually sprinkling commas over a long or convoluted sentence will not make the sentence more readable. Instead, think of commas as links or bridges between major ideas in a given sentence, whether those ideas are phrases, clauses, or single words. For example, always use a comma to link a dependent (or subordinate) clause to the independent (or main) clause in a sentence:

> Although she enjoyed chemistry, she struggled to stay awake during her Quantum Mechanics lectures.

You can also use a comma to link two independent clauses when you join those clauses with a coordinating conjunction (*and*, *but*, *or*, *nor*, *so*, *for*, *yet*). However, if the clauses are short, you may omit the comma.

> She fell asleep during most of her lectures, but she always managed to do well on the exams.

> The fire alarm sounded and the students evacuated the building.

Commas also set apart various components of the sentence from the main idea. Use a comma to set off an introductory word or contextualizing phrase.

> During their first year, many students live in residence.

> Fortunately, all residence staff are trained in conflict resolution.

In the same way, use commas to set apart words, phrases, or clauses that add extra but non-essential information to a sentence. These "by the way" or "sidebar" phrases add important details, but omitting them does not change the essential meaning of the sentence. Always frame such phrases with commas.

> When she met her assigned roommate, Bob, Shari wondered if the Residence Admissions office had made a serious mistake.

If, however, your "by the way" information is more complex—a phrase involving internal punctuation, for example—use dashes to set it off from the rest of the sentence.

> When she met her assigned roommate—Bob, the very bearded, friendly, and enthusiastically male linguistics major—Shari wondered if the Residence Admissions office had made a mistake.

As shown in the preceding example, *dashes* signal a stronger, more emphatic shift than commas do. On your keyboard, type a dash as two hyphens, with no space between the hyphens and the words involved (so as to distinguish a dash from a hyphen). In addition to setting off complex "by the way" phrases, dashes can be used to emphasize a change in thought or emotion in a sentence.

> He enjoyed going to the movies on Thursday night—but he absolutely loved attending his 8:30 am Biochemistry lecture on Fridays.

Dashes may also be used to link a list to the main part of a sentence. Although colons also serve this function, you may occasionally choose to use a dash when less formality and more emphasis seem appropriate.

> After the roadtrip, the car was crammed with evidence of a successful holiday—burger wrappers, maps, post-cards, coffee cups, ferry receipts, and one unclaimed sock.

connecting more ideas: colons and semicolons

Colons

The *colon* is the most abrupt piece of punctuation; it brings the reader to a screeching stop. Picture it as two periods, stacked. As such, it must always be preceded by an independent clause (i.e., a complete sentence), which would require a period if it were to stand on its own. The colon may be followed by a phrase, a list, a quotation, or even another independent clause.

> Remember what the road sign said: Don't Drink and Drive.

> When Jacques Villeneuve was a young boy he had one dream: he wanted to be a race car driver.

A most common use for the colon is to precede a list. However, do not use a colon when the list is a necessary part of the sentence. In grammatical terms, a colon should not be placed between a verb and its complement, or a preposition and its object. In other words, do not use a colon to break up words that function together.

> Now that she has her MBA, the dream cars that she is interested in buying are: a BMW Z3 Roadster, a Porsche Speedster 911, or a Volkswagen Carmen Ghia.

This sentence is incorrect because the colon separates the verb "are" and its complement "BMW Z3 Roadster," etc. To revise the sentence, just eliminate the colon.

> Now that she has her MBA, the dream cars that she is interested in buying are a BMW Z3 Roadster, a Porsche Speedster 911, or a Volkswagen Carmen Ghia.

Without the errant colon, the sentence is correctly punctuated.

Here is another version to consider.

> Now that she has her MBA, her dream car wish list consists of: a BMW Z3 Roadster, a Porsche Speedster 911, or a Volkswagen Carmen Ghia.

This sentence is also incorrect. In this case, the colon separates the preposition "of" and its object "BMW Z3 Roadster," etc. As above, simply omitting the colon will correct the problem.

Here's one last version.

> Now that she has her MBA, she intends to buy her dream car: a BMW Z3 Roadster, a Porsche Speedster 911, or a Volkswagen Carmen Ghia.

This is correct. The colon does not break up words that function together. Instead, it connects the list to an independent clause.

Colons should be used sparingly, especially as a means of introducing single sentence quotations in an essay. Rather, try to integrate the quotation into the syntax of your sentence. For example, although the following sentence is grammatically correct, the style is awkward.

> Hazel Motes firmly believes in his automobile: "No man with a good car needs to be justified."

Here, the colon stops the sentence too abruptly. However, in the second version of the sentence, the syntax, and hence the ideas, flows more naturally.

> As Flannery O'Connor's modernist prophet remarks, "No man with a good car needs to be justified."

On the title page of a book, the main title and subtitle are often set apart by the spacing on the page or the use of a different typeface. When citing such two-titled works in your essay, use a colon to separate the title parts.

> *Wheels: The Story of the Car in North America*

Semicolons

The *semicolon* is the most misused and misunderstood piece of punctuation. Essentially, semicolons exist only to join independent clauses (i.e., complete sentences). Noting the typographic appearance may prove helpful here: a period sits on top of a comma. The period signals that the semicolon must be preceded (and also followed) by an independent clause; the comma indicates that the semicolon intends to link related elements into a single sentence.

Sometimes, writers mistakenly use a semicolon when a comma is called for. For example, do not use a semicolon between unequal parts of a sentence, such as between independent and subordinate clauses.

> Han Solo advises R2D2 to let Chewbacca win their chess game; because Wookies are sore, and dangerous, losers.

The semicolon in this sentence is incorrect. The first clause (beginning with "Han Solo") is an independent clause and the second (beginning with "because") is a dependent clause. Use a comma instead of a colon.

> Han Solo advises R2D2 to let Chewbacca win their chess game, because Wookies are sore, and dangerous, losers.

Further, a semicolon should not appear before coordinating conjunctions—linking words such as *and*, *but*, *so*, *for*, *yet*.

> The Rebel Alliance fought valiantly; but they could not defend the Echo Base against the Imperial assault.

Here, "but" should be preceded by a comma, not a semicolon.

> The Rebel Alliance fought valiantly, but they could not defend the Echo Base against the Imperial assault.

Nevertheless, a semicolon may *take the place* of one of these joining words, lending equal conceptual weight to the linked expressions.

> Han Solo is the best blockade runner in the Outer Rim Territories; Luke Skywalker is the best starfighter in the galaxy.

In this sentence, the semicolon correctly takes the place of the coordinating conjunction *and*.

Finally, when a conjunctive adverb (such as *however*, *nevertheless*, *therefore*, *thus*) or a transitional phrase (such as *for example* or *in fact*) appears between two independent clauses in the same sentence, it must be preceded by a semicolon and is usually followed by a comma.

> Luke learns about the Force from Obi-Wan Kenobi; however, he is not told that his father has chosen to follow the Dark Side.

> Princess Leia Organa senses a mystic connection with Luke Skywalker; in fact, she is his sister.

Generally speaking, when using a semicolon, both parts of the sentence must carry equal grammatical weight; they must each be able to stand independently as a sentence if the semicolon is removed. However, there is one exception to this rule. While semicolons are never used to *introduce* a list, they are conventionally used to separate lengthy items *in* a list, especially when individual items contain internal punctuation (e.g., a comma). This convention saves confusion about which words logically belong together.

> The X-Wing Starfighter is equipped with state-of-the-art weaponry: four laser cannons, one on each wing tip; two proton torpedo launchers, placed at mid-hull; and a sophisticated targeting computer.

exclamation points!

F. Scott Fitzgerald once remarked, "An exclamation mark is like laughing at your own joke." In academic writing, use this piece of punctuation sparingly, if at all. If you feel compelled to use one, limit yourself to one. Sentences such as

> "You too could live the American Dream!!!"

come across as overblown and insincere. The author is trying too hard to make the point. Furthermore, avoid using a string of exclamation points in a string of short sentences; the effect of the exclamation point is minimized if it is overused.

> Wow! Gatsby's parties are amazing! And Daisy looks ravishing!

Never combine an exclamation point with another piece of punctuation or use it in parenthesis as an editorial comment.

> Is Daisy for real?!

> Tom claims to have studied (!) a sociological treatise.

The best practice is to avoid using the exclamation point altogether, especially in academic writing, and to rely on word choice and sentence structure to emphasize a point or express a strong feeling.

> After all the sham and corruption and human tragedy in his story, Fitzgerald still holds out hope for the American Dream.

ellipses and brackets: clarifying quoted material

When quoting external sources in your paper, you should quote only the information you need to make your point. If you intend to comment on three particular lines from a paragraph, then quote only those lines. Use an *ellipsis* to signal omissions in quoted material. Use *brackets* to insert clarifying information into a quotation.

For example, say you wanted to use the following quotation in a paper on American musical theatre but were only interested in the last few statements:

> Tony Award–winners Bernadette Peters, Joanna Gleason, and the rest of the original Broadway cast weave their magic spell over you in this masterful presentation of Stephen Sondheim's musical classic, *Into the Woods*, a seamless fusion of fairy tales that strikes at the child's heart within us all.

To omit information within the quotation, use an ellipsis (a series of three periods with a space before and after each period).

> According to one critic, "*Into the Woods* ... strikes at the child's heart within us all."

Note that the quotation *does not begin* with the ellipsis. The quotation marks are sufficient to signal the beginning of your quoted material. Use an ellipsis to indicate omissions in the middle or at the end of a quoted sentence. If you have omitted words at the end of a quoted sentence, the ellipsis must be followed by a period.

Sondheim's play centres on "a seamless fusion of fairy tales...."

You should also use an ellipsis followed by a period to signal the omission of a complete sentence in quoted material.

Sometimes, for quotations to make grammatical sense in your sentence, it is necessary to insert extra information. Use brackets (not parentheses) to add any necessary verbs or phrases to the quotation.

According to one critic, "Sondheim's musical classic, *Into the Woods*, [weaves] a seamless fusion of fairy tales that strikes at the child's heart within us all."

Note: Some instructors prefer students to place ellipses in square brackets [...] in order to distinguish them from any ellipses that may be included in the source work. In this way, brackets mark anything that the essay writer has included or excluded from the source material. Both practices, ellipses alone and ellipses in brackets, are correct. However, if the source quotation includes ellipses already—say, to indicate a pause—then any ellipses you insert into the quotation should be included in brackets, so as to distinguish them from the punctuation of the source work.

Remember, whenever you use quoted material, integrate it into the natural grammar of your sentence. Avoid free-floating quotations; instead, connect quoted material grammatically to your own writing. The integrated result (your words and the quoted material combined) should sound like a single, coherent sentence when read aloud (i.e., consistent verb tense, singulars and plurals, etc.), not like two separate sentences jammed together. Bear this in mind when punctuating, as well. Chances are, if you wouldn't include a piece of punctuation (such as a colon or comma) in the sentence if the words were all your own, you probably don't need to include it in a sentence that integrates a quotation.

contraction and possession: the apostrophe

Apostrophes signal one of two things: contraction or possession. Contractions simply squash two words together into one (or shorten one long word):

> *we will* becomes *we'll*
>
> *you are* becomes *you're*
>
> *will not* becomes *won't*
>
> *can not* or *cannot* becomes *can't*
>
> *it is* becomes *it's*

Contractions are common in casual speech and writing, but try to avoid them in formal documents such as essays, reports, etc.

Showing possession can get a little trickier. For singular nouns, just add an apostrophe plus an *s*:

> The book's cover is torn.

> I ate my housemate's leftovers.

But what if you were really hungry and helped yourself to all of the leftovers in the fridge? To show possession for a plural noun—let's assume you have several housemates—add an apostrophe after the *s*:

> I ate my housemates' leftovers.

This strategy also works for singular nouns or names that end with the letter *s*:

> Les' classes are dull.

The -*s*' strategy has traditionally been the most common form of showing possession for a word ending in *s*. However, this practice is changing. Increasingly, writers are adding a second *s* if it is actually pronounced when saying the word:

> Les's classes are dull.

This second strategy is logical, but it is still less common and may be considered an error by some readers. Use it if you're feeling grammatically brave.

apostrophes and plurals

Although apostrophes are never used to pluralize standard English words, they can be used to signal the plural of single letters:

What does it mean to mind your p's and q's?

Please note: some older usage guides advocate for an apostrophe in dates and initialisms (1990's, LP's, CD's, etc.). This is now deemed a little old-fashioned. However, whenever you encounter one of these changeable conventions, pick a strategy and stick with it. Consistency within your document is essential. And if you're still unsure about which option to choose, take your cue from other writing in your field (journal articles, texts, class handouts, etc.).

when not to use an apostrophe: possessive pronouns

Occasionally, apostrophes are unnecessary when showing possession. Words such as *mine, yours, his, hers, theirs, ours, whose,* etc., are possessive but are not spelled with an apostrophe. These are called possessive pronouns.

> <u>Whose</u> laptop is this? It's <u>hers</u>.

An important member of this elite club is the word *its*—one of the most abused and misspelled words in the language.

As discussed in Chapter 5, *its* is a possessive pronoun meaning "belonging to it." *It's* is a contraction meaning "it is" or "it has." Really. That's the rule. Every time.

seven Documentation

Nearly all academic writing will require you to use external sources, be they primary sources (statistical or experimental data, historical documents, literary works) or secondary (books or articles that interpret such primary sources). Consequently, you must accurately document these sources so that your readers will know where you got your information and be able to locate it for themselves.

Of course, locating sources is no longer a matter of looking on library shelves. Online research provides access to an enormous range of material, and, unlike hard-copy books and journals, the material itself keeps changing. A given web site can provide very different information depending on when you log on, so it is important to keep track of the date on which you accessed the site as well as the site's URL address, and, if available, the source's Digital Object Identifier (DOI) number (depending on which documentation style you choose, some or all of this information will be included in your Works Cited, References, or Bibliography page at the end of your essay). Also, the old writers' adage—"anyone can get published"—holds all the more true for online sources. Whether you are looking for information on the Web or on the shelves of the library, make sure that the information is accurate. Check the sources—both yours and theirs.

the P word: plagiarism

As you probably have heard time and time again, plagiarism is a serious form of academic dishonesty and must be avoided at all times. But what is plagiarism, exactly? By definition, plagiarism is the presentation of someone else's words or ideas as your own. Simply put, plagiarism is theft. Be it the petty larceny of a few lifted turns of phrase to the full-out fraud of submitting a bought or borrowed paper, plagiarism—whether unintentional or premeditated—is a serious academic offence. Ideas matter in academics, so stealing ideas matters a lot, too.

Still, besides avoiding plagiarism charges and their academic consequences, why do you need to cite your sources? First and foremost, citing sources gives credit to the intellectual work/property of others. It recognizes others for the work they have done. Further, citing sources helps other scholars find your source information not only to evaluate your understanding of it and the veracity of your own argument, but also, if they wish, to check out that information for themselves. Accurately representing others' words and ideas as well as citing them accurately creates a sense of transparency that is important for gaining the trust of your community of scholars. As a writer, you belong to the academic community, and academic writing functions as a part of a larger conversation. Your ideas interact with those of others to comprise the intellectual mix of your discipline. Your work is your contribution to the discourse. By citing your sources, not only do you give credit, but you also give your readers the means to engage in the interplay of ideas. Citation allows readers to find out where you got your resources and to see how your own voice and ideas fit into this larger mix.

when to cite a source

If your readers cannot distinguish between your ideas and those articulated by your source, you run the risk of plagiarizing the source material—i.e., passing off someone else's ideas as your own. This can happen when quoting, summarizing, or paraphrasing someone else's material. In each of these cases, always cite an external source.

Quoting directly

Sometimes it is appropriate to incorporate an idea from an external source directly into your paper by quoting it word for word. It may be, for example, that you want to comment specifically on the author's choice of words. It may also be that the author offers a particularly effective expression of an idea you want to use to support your argument.

You must include a citation (footnote, parenthetical reference, etc.) when quoting key words or phrases from a source. Short prose quotations (up to four lines in MLA, forty words in APA, and one hundred words in Chicago Style) should be integrated into your paragraph using quotation marks. Longer prose quotations should be indented and double-spaced; these "off-set" quotations do not require quotation marks. Similarly, poetry of one to three lines (for MLA) should be integrated into your paragraph using quotation marks and slashes to indicate the ends of lines (e.g., "Twinkle, twinkle, little star, / How I wonder what you are"). Poetry of more than three lines in MLA or two or more lines in Chicago Style should be set off from your main text—presented without quotation marks, as are other "off-set" quotations—and follow the line-by-line structure of the original poem.

Quoting specialized information

If your essay includes specific information not generally known or not likely to be found in a general reference text such as an encyclopaedia entry, that information needs to be cited. For example, most film buffs know or could easily find out that Orson Welles's landmark film *Citizen Kane* was based—not so loosely, and rather controversially—on the life of contemporary newspaper magnate William Randolph Hearst. However, they probably wouldn't know, or would not find out very easily, that prior to the film's release, a group of movie executives, fearing Hearst's wrath over the film, offered the studio $842,000 to destroy the negative and all the prints.[1] For more information on discerning between common and, for lack of a better word, uncommon knowledge, see the section below on "when not to document an external source."

Summarizing main ideas and arguments

A very effective way of using external sources is to capture, in summary form, the underlying argument, ideas, opinions, or main point of an external source. Again, be careful to assign ownership of the ideas clearly. When developing a summary, the challenge is

---

1   Pauline Kael, "Raising Kane," *The New Yorker*, 20 Feb. 1971, p. 44.

to avoid being distracted by the details. Much like when you are developing your own thesis for your essay, you must focus on the author's central argument and the assumptions underlying that argument. If you state the main argument of an external source, it may not be appropriate to cite page numbers, since that argument may play out over several pages or even chapters of the source. However, a parenthetical reference or foot- or endnote is needed if the author and title of the work are not made clear in the body of the essay. As well, you will need a citation if you paraphrase from a particular part of the text at any point in your summary.

Paraphrasing

Paraphrasing means taking someone else's idea and restating it in your own words. Doing this is trickier than it sounds. A valid paraphrase must do more than simply change or re-order a few of the author's words. The original meaning of the passage must remain intact, but the paraphrase must also be written in a way that does not borrow key phrases from the original. Finding this balance can be difficult, and many student writers—let alone graduate students and established academics—have been tripped up by sloppy or overly liberal paraphrasing. Committing plagiarism by too closely paraphrasing or summarizing the original idea or argument is a less serious infraction, but it is still plagiarism and should be avoided. As with direct quotations, always follow paraphrased information with a cited reference to the source.

For example, say you were working on a paper on women's health issues and wanted to paraphrase Barbara Ehrenreich's argument that the breast cancer support movement has evolved into "a full-fledged religion. The products—teddy bears, pink ribbon brooches, and so forth—serve as amulets and talismans, comforting the sufferer and providing visible evidence of faith."[2] A paraphrase of this statement might look like the following:

> Barbara Ehrenreich argues that the breast cancer movement has developed into a kind of religious community that provides support through its own symbols, practices, and values (50).

Note how this paraphrase captures the essence of Ehrenreich's statement without drawing from key phrases such as "full-fledged religion," "amulets and talismans," "comforting the sufferer," and "evidence of faith."

---

2   Barbara Ehrenreich, "Welcome to Cancerland," *Harper's Magazine*, vol. 303, no. 1818, Nov. 2001, p. 50.

For a more developed example, consider the following paragraph, taken from Jane Jacobs's *Dark Age Ahead*.[3]

Original

Mass amnesia, striking as it is and seemingly weird, is the least mysterious of Dark Age phenomena. We all understand the harsh principle *Use it or lose it*. A failing or conquered culture can spiral down into a long decline, as has happened in most empires after their relatively short heydays of astonishing success. But in extreme cases, failing or conquered cultures can be genuinely lost, never to emerge again as living ways of being. The salient mystery of Dark Ages sets the stage for mass amnesia. People living in vigorous cultures typically treasure those cultures and resist any threat to them. How and why can a people so totally discard a formerly vital culture that it becomes literally lost?

A "Too-Close Paraphrase" (Note the similarity of the words in bold)

Jacobs notes that **mass amnesia** is the **weirdest**, but **least mysterious aspect** of a Dark Age. Most people understand the phrase **use it or lose it**, and know that

_____

3   Jane Jacobs, *Dark Age Ahead*, Random House Canada, 2004, p. 4.

cultures can go into **decline** when they stray from the culture that made them **successful** in the first place. But **how do peoples lose** or dispose of an entire culture especially ones that were once vibrant and safe (4)?

In this paraphrase, the writer manages to condense the ideas found in the original passage but draws too much on the original language to make the point. Not only are the ideas Jacobs's, but the central expression of them is hers as well. The writer has borrowed too much and has, whether intentionally or not, plagiarized. Try again.

Acceptable Paraphrase

"Mass Amnesia," a process by which previously vibrant cultures irrecoverably disappear, characterizes what Jacobs calls "Dark Ages." While she is not surprised that many cultures in crisis, including the majority of empires, have gradually diminished over time, she finds the complete loss of a culture remarkable. Jacobs wonders what can motivate a loyal people to abandon a culture they once valued greatly (4).

Here the writer has done a better job. The points at which the writer uses some of Jacobs's key terms ("mass amnesia," "Dark Age") are closely aligned to the source writer ("what Jacobs calls") and put in double quotation marks. The rest of the paraphrase manages to summarize Jacobs's points accurately and succinctly, using original language. Note that an acceptable paraphrase can repeat common words ("culture," "people," "empires") that are central to the original and for which there are no reasonable substitutes.

when not to cite a source

Sometimes you will include in your writing information that is understood to be *common knowledge* (for example, the fact that World War II ended in 1945). In this case, you do not need to cite a source. However, any opinions, interpretations, or evaluations of that common knowledge information must be documented.

Also, bear in mind that common knowledge is often discourse-specific. In other words, what is held to be common knowledge in your Religious Studies class may not be so common in Psychology 101 or your World Cinema course; there may even be discrepancies between different courses within a given discipline. Use your classroom experience as a guide. If a piece of information would be understood without a reference in class discussion, consider it common knowledge. If not, cite your source.

documentation systems

The format of any in-text documentation depends on the system you are using. The most commonly used documentation systems are MLA (Modern Language Association) for arts and humanities papers, and APA (American Psychological Association) for writing in social and health sciences. Each of these systems uses parenthetical citations that include a combination of author and either date or page number information. Foregoing parenthetical citations for footnotes or endnotes and a bibliography, however, is one of the methods outlined in the *Chicago Manual of Style*. History departments often prefer this "Chicago Style." All disciplines have certain assumptions and expectations regarding documentation style, and these standards can vary from subject to subject. Check with your instructor or marker to make sure that you are using an appropriate documentation method.

Ultimately, the most important rule for documentation is consistency. Use a clear, appropriate format, and use it in the same way throughout your paper. Generally speaking, your documentation will combine references to the author and work in the body of your essay using parenthetical references or footnotes/endnotes. These references will then be fully cited in a separate Works

Cited (or References or Bibliography) page at the end of your essay. The following section, a general guide outlining the kinds of information to include and the order in which to include it, provides formatting examples for many common situations. In cases where you do not have all the information given in the example—perhaps your document does not list an author—just skip that element and include the rest of the information in sequence. For more comprehensive or specialized examples, consult the full guide for the system you are using. For information on documenting sources in scientific disciplines, see Chapter Nine, "Writing in the Sciences."

MODERN LANGUAGE ASSOCIATION (MLA) FORMAT

MLA format, commonly used for humanities and arts papers, uses parenthetical citations for in-text referencing. These citations usually follow an "author page #" format (Hardy 295). However, "title page #" is also acceptable if it offers greater clarity, as would be the case in an English Literature essay that considered several works by a single author. For example, an essay about Thomas Hardy's *Tess of the D'Urbervilles* and *Jude the Obscure* would be better cited as (*Tess* 295) and (*Jude* 452), since Hardy's authorship would be understood by the reader. Other resources in the essay, such as journal articles, would be cited using the "author page #" format. For electronic and other non-print sources, use the name that begins your Works Cited entry. If the web site does not use page numbers, check to see if the paragraphs or screens are numbered and use that information instead. For example, try (Korba, par. 27) or (Korba, screens 2–3). The more clearly and succinctly you can get your reader to the information, the better. In all MLA style papers, full bibliographic information is included in a Works Cited section at the end of the essay, and all citations are listed alphabetically by author (or by title, in the case of anonymous sources).

Double space the Works Cited list, and give each entry in it a hanging indent.

Since electronic documents are not fixed entities, referencing them requires particular attention to detail. In your research and writing it is crucial that you note the date you accessed the material, the date of its last revision, and any sponsoring agencies of the site or database. Check to see if there is an author or a title for the particular page or document you are referencing. All this information is needed for your Works Cited section. Finally, note the site's complete URL or DOI (electronic address), which should be your citation's penultimate item (prior to the date accessed).

in-text citations

Direct quotation

"Semicolons are often undervalued" (Markham 172).

Paraphrase

Many attach little importance to the semicolon (Markham 172).

Two or more sources by the same author

"Semicolons are often undervalued" (Markham, *Grammar* 172).

[Note: "*Grammar*" is a shortened version of the book's full title: *Grammar: The Key to Happiness and Power*.]

Source with multiple authors

"It is high time that we revisit the role of the hyphen" (Markham and Caffrey 514).

Edited, multi-volume source with more than three editors

"Clearly, semicolons have been undervalued for centuries" (Markham et al. 2: 147).

Poetry

"Artful link / Of independent clauses" (Markham 23-24).

Play

"I've had enough of this semicolon nonsense. I'm leaving" (Markham 3.1.45-46).

Indirect source (quoting an author whose words appear in a second source)

In *Memoirs*, Markham confesses, "I never understood parentheses" (qtd. in Caffrey 63).

works cited

Book by one author

Markham, Howard. *Grammar: The Key to Happiness and Power*. Stuart & Stuart, 2012.

——. *Grammatical Foundations for a Better Society*. Smith & Jones, 2016. *The Howard Markham Online Archive*, www.howardmarkham.ca. Accessed 23 Mar. 2017.

Anthology or compilation

Caffrey, Liz, ed. *The Complete Howard Markham*. Progressive, 2009, 5 vols.

Multiple authors

[two authors:] Caffrey, Liz, and Howard Markham. *Reinventing Grammar*. Stuart & Stuart, 2016.

[three or more authors:] Campbell, Peter, et al. *Punctuation with Power*. Oxbow, 2015.

Editions other than the first

Markham, Howard. *Grammar: The Key to Happiness and Power*. 3rd ed., Stuart & Stuart, 2012.

Introduction (also applies to foreword or preface)

Caffrey, Liz. Introduction. *Memoirs*, by Howard Markham, Grant Brothers, 2010, pp. ii–vii.

Work in an anthology

Markham, Howard. "Comma Splices and Other Crimes." *Masterworks of Minor Consequence*, edited by Liz Caffrey, 4th ed., vol. 3, Progressive, 2015, pp. 47–61.

Translation

Marceau, Julie. *Language Anxiety*. Translated by Liz Caffrey, Éditions linguistiques, 2011.

Article in a newspaper

Caffrey, Liz. "Small Publishers Hit the Big Time." *Kingston This Week*, 14 May 2015, Ontario ed., pp. A12–13.

——. "Semicolons and Good Citizenship: Is There a Link?" *Writing Daily*, 9 Jan. 2011, n. pag., www.writingdaily.ca. Accessed 21 Feb. 2017.

Article in a magazine published monthly

Caffrey, Liz. "Small Publishers Hit the Big Time." *Back Issues*, May 2015, pp. 14–17.

——. "A Grammar Maven's Life." *Good Grammar to You*. The Good Grammar Group, June 2010, n. pag, www.goodgrammargroup.com. Accessed 16 Sept. 2016.

Article in a scholarly journal

Caffrey, Liz. "Why Howard Markham Matters More Than We Think." *Grammar in Canada*, vol. 27, 2014, pp. 205–27.

——. "Markham on the Apostrophe: A Neglected Gem." *Annals of Punctuation*, vol. 35, no. 3, 2009, pp. 114–37, doi:10.9876/ap.12345.67. Accessed 29 Mar. 2017.

Book review

Caffrey, Liz. "Salvific Grammar." Review of *Grammar: The Key to Happiness and Power*, by Howard Markham, *Kingston Review of Books*, 23 Oct. 2016, n. pag., www.kingstonreview.ca/br/2016-10-23. Accessed 3 Dec. 2016.

Article in a reference book

"Semicolon." *Markham-Caffrey Collegiate Dictionary*, 13th ed., 2016.

Markham, Howard. "Conjunctive Adverbs through the Ages." *Encyclopaedia Kingstonia Online*, 15th ed., 2009, www.encyclopaediakingstonia.ca. Accessed 10 Mar. 2017.

Film

Bad Fiction. Directed by Quentin Caffrey, performances by John Markham and Uma Caffrey, Educational Media Resources, 2017.

Television broadcast

"Splendid Semicolons." *The Language and Grammar Hour*, produced by Howard Markham, The Punctuation Channel, 4 Aug. 2016.

Lecture or speech

Caffrey, Quentin. "Grammar on Film." Annual General Meeting, Society for Technical Details, 13 Oct. 2016, Kingston Public Library, Kingston, ON. Lecture.

Interview

Clarke, Lynne. Personal interview. 4 Aug. 2016.

Web site

Caffrey, Liz. "FAQs and Arguments." *Grammar Forum Home Page*, The Markham Institute for Higher Punctuation, 9 Dec. 2014, www.mihp.ca/grammarforum. Accessed 15 Apr. 2017.

Blog post

CommaGuy1515 [Josh Smith]. "Re: Using the Oxford Comma," *PunctuationNow*, 29 Mar. 2017, punctuationnow.com/comma/oxford/ongoing_saga. Accessed 15 Apr. 2017.

Tweet

Markham, Howard (hmarkham2189). "Use a hyphen!" 16 Apr. 2017, 8:05 PM. Tweet.

Email

Caffrey, Liz. "Re: When to use a semicolon." Received by Howard Markham, 6 Apr. 2017.

AMERICAN PSYCHOLOGICAL ASSOCIATION (APA) FORMAT

APA format is used primarily for papers in the social sciences. Like MLA format, it calls for in-text parenthetical citations, but with an author-date rather than author-page number focus, e.g., (Chomsky, 1987). When an author's name appears within the text rather than within parentheses, the source's date follows immediately in parentheses, as here: "Chomsky (1987) maintains that...." The citations for direct quotations must also include a page number reference (Chomsky, 1987, p. 56). For sources without pagination, citations include instead a paragraph or heading reference (Chomsky, 1987, para. 5), (Chomsky, 1987, Summary of conclusions). Full bibliographic information is arranged alphabetically by author surname (or by title for works with no identified author) at the end of a paper, in a list titled References. For authors' first names, give initials only. Double-space the References list, and give each entry in it a hanging indent. Personal communications should appear in-text only, not in References. If your source has a Digital Object Identifier (DOI—a string of numbers and punctuation beginning with 10, usually located on the first or copyright page), include it at the end of the References entry (e.g., doi:10.1098/6889-4673.55.3.989). For electronic sources that do not have a DOI, include the URL (Web address) at the entry's end (e.g., Retrieved from http://www.markhamonline.com).

in-text citations

Direct quotation

"Semicolons are often undervalued" (Markham, 2016, p. 172).

Markham (2016) asserts that "semicolons are often undervalued" (p. 172).

Direct quotation from an online source with no pagination

"Surprisingly little work has been done on the social effects of apostrophe abuse" (Markham, 2008, para. 4).

More than one source by the same author

"Semicolons are often undervalued" (Markham, 2016b, p. 172).

Source with multiple authors

"It is high time that we revisit the role of the hyphen" (Markham & Caffrey, 2016).

When referring to three or more authors, list each author in the first reference, and then use "et al." ("and others") in subsequent references: (Markham et al., 2017).

Source with no identified author

Cite a shortened version of the work's title; here, the reference is to the article "Perspectives on Punctuation":

Confusion between hyphens and dashes has been clearly documented for decades ("Perspectives," 2017).

Citing several sources in one place

Many usage guides overemphasize particular points of grammar (Caffrey, 2016; Markham, 2016).

Personal communication

Many usage guides overemphasize particular points of grammar (L. Caffrey, personal communication, February 28, 2017).

[In APA format, personal communication refers to non-retrievable documents, such as email, interviews, and correspondence conducted or received by the author of the paper. Such sources appear only in the body of the text and not in a list of references.]

Secondary source (quoting an author whose words or ideas appear in a second source)

In *Memoirs*, Markham (2008) confesses, "I never understood parentheses" (as cited in Caffrey, p. 63).

APA references

Article in a scholarly journal

Markham, H. (2017). Comma splices and other crimes. *Journal of Canadian Languages, 24*, 67–81. doi:10.1065/4000679.34.87009

[Note that volume numbers are put in italics, and no period comes after a DOI.]

Article in a journal in which each issue begins on page 1

Give the issue number in parentheses right after the volume number:

Caffrey, L. (2016). Markham on the apostrophe: A neglected gem. *Annals of Punctuation, 35*(3) (2009): 114–137. doi:10.1098/0016-445.78.3.977

Article in a magazine

Markham, H., & Caffrey, L. (2017, November). Grammar for the new millennium. *Nerds Monthly, 26*, 35–52.

Caffrey, L. (2016, June). A grammar maven's life. *Good Grammar Today 44*(2). Retrieved from http://www.gram.org/goodgrammartoday.com

Article in a newspaper

Syntax scandal hits city hall. (2015, April 1). *The Daily Nerd*, p. A12.

Caffrey, L. (2018, January 9). Semicolons and good citizenship: Is there a link? *Writing Daily*. Retrieved from http://www.wdaily.com

Book by one author

Markham, H. (2016). *Grammar: The key to happiness and power*. Kingston, ON: Stuart and Stuart.

Markham, H. (2017). *Grammatical foundations for a better society*. The Howard Markham online archive. Retrieved from http://www.howardmarkham.com

Multiple authors

Caffrey, L., & Markham, H. (2016). *Reinventing grammar*. Toronto: Academic Press.

Campbell, P., Aleksiuk, N., & Cole, A. (2015). *Punctuation with power*. Buffalo, NY: Oxbow.

Anthology or compilation

Caffrey, L. (Ed.). (2009). *The complete Howard Markham*. New York & London: Progressive.

Work in an anthology

Markham, H. (2015). Comma splices and other crimes. In L. Caffrey (Ed.), *Masterworks of minor consequence* (pp. 132–145). New York & London: Progressive Press.

Introduction (also applies to foreword or preface)

Cole, A. (2015). Introduction. In L. Caffrey (Ed.), *The complete Howard Markham* (pp. 4–13). New York & London: Progressive Press.

Book, edition other than the first

Caffrey, L., & Markham H., Jr. (2017). *Punctuating the social sciences: A beginner's guide* (3rd ed.). Kingston, ON: Stuart and Stuart.

Translation

Marceau, J. (2016). *Language anxiety*. (L. Caffrey, Trans.). Montreal: Éditions linguistiques.

Book review

Caffrey, L. (2018, January 16). Grammar as a mood enhancer. [Review of the book *Grammar: The key to happiness and power*, by H. Markham]. *Writing and Psychology Quarterly, 103*(2). doi:10.1123/000-987.47.9.0006

Entry in a print reference work

Markham, H. (2017). Punctuation therapy. In L. Caffrey (Ed.), *The encyclopaedia of cognitive punctuation*. Kingston, ON: Stuart and Stuart.

Entry in an online reference work, no author or editor, no date

Social grammar theory. (n.d.). In *Grammar dictionary online* (12th ed.). Retrieved from http://www.grammar.com/dictionary/socio/

Television broadcast

Markham, H. (Executive Producer). (2017, February 27). *The language and grammar hour* [Television broadcast]. Kingston, ON: Stuartville Broadcasting Corporation.

Film

Caffrey, Q. (Director), & Markham, J. (Producer). (2017). *Bad fiction* [Motion picture]. Canada: Educational Media Resources.

Web site

Caffrey, L. (2017, April 15). FAQs and arguments. Retrieved from http://www.grammarforum.org

---

CHICAGO MANUAL OF STYLE (CHICAGO STYLE) FORMAT

The Chicago Manual of Style outlines two basic documentation systems: one is similar to the APA style, and the other uses notes (footnotes or endnotes) and a bibliography to document sources. It is this second system, the one that uses a **footnote** or **endnote** style of referencing, that we call "Chicago Style." In Chicago Style, superscript numbers in your text direct the reader to a note entry, either at the bottom of the page (footnote) or in a Notes section at the end of your paper (endnote). At the very end of your paper comes a Bibliography, which lists not only all the sources you have referred to in your footnotes or endnotes but also every source you have consulted. Arrange the entries alphabetically by authors' last names; if no author or editor is identified, alphabetize the entry by the title. Give each entry a hanging indent.

some models for footnotes or endnotes

The first references to secondary sources include full details. The rules of what to include in those details can vary depending on what kind of source you are referring to. Note also that the form changes slightly between the footnote/endnote and the bibliography entry.

The models below show formats for citing a source for the first time. In additional references to the same book, article, etc., use only the author's last name and a page number in your note: 3. Babington, 36. If you are citing two works by the same author, include the title as well in second and subsequent notes: 7. Babington, *Meeting and Greeting*, 316. If you are citing two writers with the same last name, include the initial to avoid confusion: 16. R. Babington, *Hunting and Gathering*, 188.

When citing an online source, include at the end of the note and bibliography entry the site's URL (Web address) or, preferably, the Digital Object Identifier (DOI)—if one is available, it is a string of numbers and punctuation beginning with 10, usually located on the first or copyright page (e.g., doi:10.1098/6889-4673.55.3.989). Whether or not you include a URL or DOI, end each note and bibliography entry with a period. Chicago style does not require writers to include the dates on which they accessed online material, but check with your instructors; some may wish you to record those dates. Add them before the URL or DOI, after the word *accessed*.

Book by one author, first edition—print and e-book formats

Footnote/Endnote

> 1. Rudolf B. Babington, *Hunting and Gathering* (Kingston, ON: Stuart and Stuart, 2017), 54.

> 1. Rudolf B. Babington, *Hunting and Gathering* (Kingston, ON: Stuart and Stuart, 2017), Kobo edition, chap. 14.

[Because the pagination of electronic books depends on the size of the text, which can be variable, cite chapter or section rather than page numbers.]

Bibliography entry

> Babington, Rudolf B. *Hunting and Gathering.* Kingston, ON: Stuart and Stuart, 2017.

> Babington, Rudolf B. *Hunting and Gathering.* Kingston, ON: Stuart and Stuart, 2017. Kobo edition.

Later edition of a book

Footnote/Endnote

> 2. Tom Carpenter, *Carpentry*, 2nd. ed. (Toronto: Woodworkers International, 2015), 207.

Bibliography entry

Carpenter, Tom. *Carpentry*. 2nd. ed. Toronto: Wood-
workers International, 2015.

Book by two or three authors

Footnote/Endnote

3. Susan Fowler and Susan Korba, *Achieving Greatness
in Film Studies* (Hollywood, CA: Cinematic Press, 2017),
12.

Bibliography entry

Fowler, Susan, and Susan Korba. *Achieving Greatness in
Film Studies*. Hollywood, CA: Cinematic Press, 2017.

For a third author, follow this example:

3. Peter Campbell, Natasha Aleksiuk, and Andrea
Cole.

The bibliography entry would look like this:

Campbell, Peter, Natasha Aleksiuk, and Andrea Cole.

Book with both an author and an editor or translator

Footnote/Endnote

4. Joy Obadia, *Lost in Translation*, trans. and ed. Stella
Spriet (Vancouver: Smith Brothers, 2016), 112.

Bibliography entry

Obadia, Joy. *Lost in Translation*. Translated and edited by Stella Spriet. Vancouver: Smith Brothers, 2016.

Anthology

Footnote/Endnote

5. Peter Clandfield and David Stymeist, eds., *Poetical Works of RMC*, 2nd ed., vol. 2 (Kingston, ON: Stuart and Stuart, 2018), 1009.

Bibliography entry

Clandfield, Peter, and David Stymeist, eds. *Poetical Works of RMC*. 2nd ed. Vol. 2. Kingston, ON: Stuart and Stuart, 2018.

Chapter in an edited collection

Footnote/Endnote

6. Kevin Brushett, "The Culture of Kingston West," in *Ontario: Studies in Futility*, ed. Donna Katinas and F.M. Garvie, 1213–19 (Kingston, ON: Stuart and Stuart, 2016), 1214.

Bibliography entry

Brushett, Kevin. "The Culture of Kingston West." In *Ontario: Studies in Futility*, edited by Donna Katinas and F.M. Garvie, 1213–19. Kingston, ON: Stuart and Stuart, 2016.

Introduction (also applies to foreword or preface)

Footnote/Endnote

7. Liz Caffrey, introduction to *Memoirs*, by Howard Markham (Columbus, OH: Grant Brothers, 2018).

Bibliography entry

Caffrey, Liz. Introduction to *Memoirs*, by Howard Markham. Columbus, OH: Grant Brothers, 2018.

Article in a scholarly journal

Footnote/Endnote

8. Sandy Bugeja, "Transactional Theory: Against Dualisms," *Queen's English* 54 (2016): 380.

9. Leslie Casson, "Thirteen Ways of Looking at Kingston Rhetoric," *Queen's Notes Quarterly* 112, no. 2 (2016): 45–67, accessed March 5, 2011, doi:10.1179/448.03255.

[If each issue of a volume begins with page 1, include the issue number, as above.]

Bibliography entry

Bugeja, Sandy. "Transactional Theory: Against Dualisms." *Queen's English* 54 (2016): 380–401.

Casson, Leslie. "Thirteen Ways of Looking at Kingston Rhetoric." *Queen's Notes Quarterly* 112, no.2 (2016): 45–67. Accessed March 5, 2011. doi:10.1179/448.03255.

Book review

Footnote/Endnote

10. Douglas Babington, review of *The Limits of Patience*, by Martina Hardwick, *Napanee Journal of Sociolinguistics* 91 (2017): 727.

Bibliography entry

Babington, Douglas. Review of *The Limits of Patience*, by Martina Hardwick. *Napanee Journal of Sociolinguistics* 91 (2017): 726–27.

Article in a magazine

Footnote/Endnote

11. Liz Caffrey, "Small Publishers Hit the Big Time," *Back Issues*, May 2017, 14–17.

Bibliography entry

Caffrey, Liz. "Small Publishers Hit the Big Time." *Back Issues*, May 2017, 14–17.

Article in a newspaper

Footnote/Endnote

12. Rosalind Malcolm, "200th Birthday of Grimms Celebrated," *Toronto Bugle*, March 15, 2017, sec. 1A, p. 3.

13. Kevin Brushett, "Writing Tutors in High Demand," *Kingston Times*, January 29, 2018, http://www.Kingstontimes.com/2011/01/29/news/02.html.

Bibliography entry

Malcolm, Rosalind. "200th Birthday of Grimms Celebrated." *Toronto Bugle*, March 15, 2017, sec. 1A, p. 3.

Brushett, Kevin. "Writing Tutors in High Demand." *Kingston Times*, January 29, 2018. http://www.Kingstontimes.com/2011/01/29/news/02.html.

[For newspaper articles, page and section numbers may be omitted, but if you do include them, follow the format in the first sample above. The "p." is used to make clear the difference between the page and section numbers.]

Entry in a reference book

Footnote/Endnote

14. *Encyclopaedia Kingstonia*, 11th ed., s.v. "Whales," by E. Johnson and R. May.

14. *Encyclopaedia Kingstonia Online*, 11th ed., s.v. "Whales," by E. Johnson and R. May, accessed August 7, 2017.

Bibliography entry

Encyclopaedia Kingstonia. 11th ed. 3 vols. Kingston: Cataraqui Press, 2008.

Encyclopaedia Kingstonia Online. 11th ed. Accessed August 7, 2017. http://kingstonrefs/entries/whales/.

[The s.v., for Latin *sub verbo*, means "under the word."]

Interview by writer of the research paper

Footnote/Endnote

15. Lynne Clarke, interview by author, Kingston, ON, May 1, 2017.

Bibliography entry

Clarke, Lynne. Interview by author. Kingston, ON, May 1, 2017.

[Note that "author" refers to the person writing the paper and who performed the interview; "Lynne Clarke" is the subject of that interview and is the person being quoted.]

Lecture

Footnote/Endnote

16. Quentin Caffrey, "Grammar on Film" (lecture, Annual General Meeting, Society for Technical Details, Kingston Public Library, Kingston, ON, 13 Oct. 2017).

Bibliography entry

Caffrey, Quentin. "Grammar on Film." Lecture presented at the Annual General Meeting, Society for Technical Details, Kingston Public Library, Kingston, ON, 13 Oct. 2017.

Web site

Footnote/Endnote

17. Paul Gamache, "Zen and the Art of Writing for the Internet." Zen Public Library, http://www.writethisdown.org/zen/zen-1.0_toc.html (accessed June 4, 2017).

Bibliography entry

Gamache, Paul. "Zen and the Art of Writing for the Internet." Zen Public Library. Accessed June 4, 2017. http://www.writethisdown.org/zen/zen-1.0_toc.html.

eight Business Writing

When writing for business—be it for Business, Commerce, or MBA studies or for projects in the workplace—the primary focus is twofold: practicality and precision. Business writing always seeks to accomplish something: it reports, persuades, sells, evaluates, summarizes, proposes, responds, inquires. In this arena, the act of writing is always a means to an end, a way of communicating a precise message to a specific audience. In this way, business writing is extremely practical. Every communication, whether email, letter, memo, or report, needs a clear objective. To meet this practical demand, business writers must communicate their message as precisely and concisely as possible. Vague or unfocused writing literally wastes the reader's time, and in North American business culture especially, time is money. And wasting either—time or money—is a bad career move. Unlike the expansive theoretical writing common to other disciplines, business writing forces the writer to boil things down to the essentials. When in doubt, keep it simple and keep it short.

reader-centred writing: it's all about you

Business writing accentuates its message by focusing squarely on the reader. The reader's needs are always emphasized over and above those of the writer. This strategy doesn't eliminate the writer's agenda, however. Consider the following statement:

> We will not accept applications after April 15th.

In this statement, the emphasis is entirely writer-centred. The content of the sentence focuses on the application deadline—the thing that matters most to the company sending the letter. *We have a deadline, and we will stick to it without exception*, the statement implies. *We* have something *you* want, and if *you* want to apply, then *you* have to do what *we* say. This approach forces the reader into a passive position. The writer is in control. However, with a little tweaking, this same message can take on a reader-centred focus.

> Please send us your application by April 15th.

Here, in an effort to personalize the content and encourage an active response, the writer has addressed the reader directly. The revised statement communicates the same information, but it does so in a way that draws the reader in. The deadline has not changed, but the tone has. Now the reader has the power—he or she has the application that the writer is asking to see. There is still a deadline, but that detail is secondary to the company's enthusiasm to receive the application. By focusing on the reader's needs (to be encouraged, to be invited), the writer manages to communicate the same information in a way that motivates the reader to respond.

always look on the bright side: making negatives positive

The above revision also shows the value of positive language. Rather than focus on what cannot be done (submitting an application after April 15th) the writer emphasizes what *can*—submitting by April 15th. Keeping things positive helps the writer to maintain an open, active relationship with the reader. Negatives shut down possibilities; positives create them. Whenever possible, try to frame your information in a positive light. Focus on what *is* happening or what *is* possible rather than dwell solely on what didn't or won't work. For example, consider the following statements from a progress report:

> The design engineers failed to take wind shear into account, stalling tower construction by several months.

> The project has experienced some delays; however, as soon as the design engineers finalize the wind shear calculations, Phase Two construction will move ahead.

The first sentence focuses on what failed. It blames the engineers and emphasizes the delay, leaving the reader with a negative impression of the project. The second sentence acknowledges the bad news (the project is behind schedule) but emphasizes what has been done to remedy the situation. Rather than criticize the engineers for messing things up, the writer focuses on what is being done to improve the situation. The reader is left with the impression that the people involved in the project are solving problems and moving forward.

Of course, not every writing situation is a positive one. Sometimes, business writers have to deliver bad news—projects fail, applications get rejected, employees get fired. In these cases, try to find a positive approach without sounding disingenuous. For example, firing an employee by saying

> We are confident that this dismissal will open up exciting new employment opportunities for you

is a bit ridiculous. False optimism is both irritating and insulting. Something more plain spoken—direct and respectful—would better suit the occasion.

Your efforts in the finance department have not gone unnoticed. We have appreciated your commitment to the company softball team, the lunchroom potluck schedule, and the Chairman's Committee on Casual Fridays.

However, your involvement with the recent Christmas Party debacle and the resulting criminal investigation leaves us with little choice but to terminate your employment, effective immediately.

Whenever possible, try to express bad news in a constructive manner. Just not at the expense of credibility.

creating information snapshots: parallel structure

In addition to adopting a reader-centred prose style, business writers should create a reader-friendly visual style as well. Most day-to-day business documents are read quickly, often skimmed for key information. Emails, memos, and short reports need to provide a kind of information snapshot; the reader should be able to glean the details in a brief glance. This imperative affects the style and structure of business documents.

For example, when creating a list (of actions or concepts), it is important to express these ideas using *parallel structure*. Parallel structure simply means expressing each idea in a way that echoes, or parallels, the other items in the list. Say you were drafting your résumé and wanted to detail the work you did as a group leader at a summer camp. Start first by brainstorming all aspects of the job experience:

- lifeguard
- supervising the campers—stayed in cabins with children (ages 8–14) for 4 two-week camp sessions
- first-aid training ... (it came in handy the morning that Betty choked on her pancakes on the overnight canoe trip)
- coordinated activities for Parents' Visitation Day (campers, staff, and parents numbered about 250 people)
- taught swimming and canoeing with 3 other group leaders

This is a good start. Once you have the main ideas down, think about how best to express them in a parallel manner. This usually involves deciding if it is best to describe them as actions (expressed as verbs) or concepts (expressed as nouns). In this case, "taught swimming" describes an action but "lifeguard" is the name of one of your roles at the camp. See if you can describe the ideas in a parallel fashion—focusing either on verbs (what you did) or on nouns (what you were).

The noun approach might look like the following:

- lifeguard
- group leader
- first-aid provider
- activity coordinator
- swimming and canoeing instructor

The noun approach is useful if your audience is familiar with the concepts in your list. In other words, if you know that your audience will understand all that is involved in being a "lifeguard" or an "activity coordinator," then listing your job by role might be an efficient strategy.

However, in the above list, some of the things listed don't lend themselves very well to this kind of expression. For example, you had to administer first aid—you had to perform an action—when Betty choked on her pancakes; expressing that action as "first-aid provider" is a little awkward, if not downright confusing. Further, it is possible that the people reading your résumé have never been to summer camp and thus may not know what an activity coordinator really does. In this case, it would probably be better to list things as actions—as verbs. That way, your description will focus on what you did, and those action words might paint a more accurate picture of your experience (and your skill-set) for your reader. Try expressing each idea as a kind of action. Think of your list as a series of sentences beginning with the word "I," as in "As a camp leader/lifeguard, I ..."

- provided lifeguarding support for waterfront activities
- supervised campers, aged 8–14, during 14-day residential camping programs
- administered first aid, in both emergency and non-emergency situations
- coordinated activities for up to 250 campers, staff, and parents on weekly Parent Visitation Day
- taught swimming and canoeing

Often, particularly in the case of résumés, listing things as verbs is both easier and more informative. Verbs provide the reader with a clear, active account of what happened. In many cases, they offer a more active snapshot of the information than nouns or concepts can. Regardless of the form you use, however, make sure that it is expressed using parallel structure. In the example above, not only is the emphasis on the action described, but the verb is the first word in each entry. This structure tells the reader that you "provided, supervised, administered, coordinated, and taught" in your job. The structure creates a logical and visual rhythm, and this rhythm makes the information easier to grasp. The reader does not have to go looking for the core content. Instead, the ideas are laid out clearly and accessibly.

creating more information snapshots: bullets and headings

When dealing with documents like résumés, reports, and memos, think also about visual presentation. Creating an information snapshot also means organizing the information in a way that is visually efficient, and in business writing, that efficiency often comes in the form of bulleted lists or headings. For instance, even though it would be grammatically sound and likely very interesting to explain the previous camp counsellor information in a long prose paragraph, this approach would be inefficient. Reading long prose passages is time consuming and requires intense concentration. The reader must sift and sort through the data, deciding (based on the writer's cues) which information is central, which is supplementary, and so on. Bullets and headings, however, provide a more transparent structure. By highlighting the key points, bullets and headings do a little bit of the cognitive heavy-lifting, enabling the reader to process more information more quickly.

Nevertheless, bulleted lists or headings cannot be used indiscriminately. They may offer a few short-cuts for the reader, but they must not be used as shortcuts for the writer. If you're not sure how things fit together, stringing things together with headings or in bullets will not help. The bullets or headings must make sense—the relationships among them must be intuitive, both to you and to your reader. Similarly, using too many bullets or headings can pose a problem: too many, and your document can end up feeling fragmented and disjointed; too few, and their purpose is unclear. As a writer, it is your job to make sure that the reader can make the necessary connections between ideas.

Also, when dealing with bullets in particular, it is important to consider how these features appear on the page. Is the bulleting style consistent? Is there adequate white space between the bullets or are they all crammed in together? Are there several different kinds of bullets on the page (bullets within bullets, with different symbols attached, etc.)? Remember, bullets help sort information. Bombarding your reader with a symphony of dots, dashes, and asterisks often just creates visual noise. Used to excess, the graphics can draw so much attention to themselves, and to the act of sorting among them, that the ideas they structure, and the rhythm that connects them, get lost. As with your prose style, so it is with bullets. When in doubt, keep it simple.

memos, letters, and reports: conventional formats

Business writers also create information snapshots by using common formats and templates for everyday business communication. Conventional formats for memos and reports help writers structure their ideas. These templates provide a ready-made logical framework for the writer. As well, presenting information in a consistent fashion helps the reader. If the logical structure of a document is transparent, then the reader can access the information efficiently. Of course, these templates are merely conventions; they are not fixed structures that apply to all situations. As with all other writing, the content and purpose of your document will define its structure, as will the context for writing. If you are not sure about conventional formatting for a given situation, look at how other similar documents are structured. Take your cues from your context—memos, letters, and reports written by more experienced colleagues may help you figure out how to format your own project. As well, a quick search will lead you to innumerable templates and examples on-line. The following discussion offers a bit of a primer on the logic behind these standard forms.

Memos

Memos are brief internal documents intended to offer the reader short updates, announcements, summaries, etc. Occasionally, memo contents are multi-faceted (a regular monthly update of miscellaneous information from Human Resources, for example), but most of the time, they address a single matter and are usually communicated via email.

For this reason, the actual content of the memo is kept very brief. When writing the "subject" line, try to be as precise as possible. A subject line that simply says "Staff Update" could refer to anything. On the other hand, one that reads "Staffing Changes, Finance Department" gives the reader a clearer idea of what is to come.

When composing the body of the memo, precision and clarity are crucial. The information contained must be concise but complete, outlining the purpose of the memo, the pertinent background or contextual details, and the action required in response. Try structuring your content with these three sections in mind: purpose, details, and action. The opening and closing sections—the purpose statement and the action statement—should stand as single paragraphs, 1–3 sentences in length. The purpose statement tells the reader why the memo is being written. The action statement tells the reader what is required or requested of him or her in response to the memo. The middle section outlines any necessary descriptive, contextualizing, or background details, and it may include several short paragraphs, bulleted lists, and/or headings.

Business letters

While memos are intended for internal communication, business letters are usually external—letters to clients, shareholders, customers, applicants, etc. When composing a business letter, keep your audience in mind. Make sure your letter has a clear objective, gives appropriate details, and encourages a clear response from the reader. As with the action statement of a memo, that response can be very simple. For example, a general letter to bank customers might end with an encouragement to "apply for your new line of credit before October 1st." Though simple, this statement still encourages a concrete response. Business communication encourages action—it gives the reader not only a reason to read the letter, but a way to respond to it as well.

In all cases, remember to maintain a courteous and professional tone. Be friendly, but not casual. If the letter brings bad news, be direct but not angry. Business letters are just that: business letters; avoid taking on a personal emotional tone. An overly familiar tone, like an overly critical one, can distract the reader from the content. Make your case, but make it from an appropriate professional stance.

Reports

Business reports have many purposes. They can offer progress updates for an ongoing project, report on activities (such as a conference or meeting), or provide a detailed overview of a subject. Their scope can vary from a brief memo or email message to a book-length document that includes appendices, graphics, chapters, and references. In general, the formality of a report is tied to its scope: the longer and more detailed the report, the more formal its presentation.

Reports are usually structured by headings. These provide a map of the contents and allow the reader to navigate the report information more efficiently. The content of a given report—its purpose and scope—will define the headings you use. For example, a progress report will likely involve separate sections concerning the background of the project, current status or activities, goals or schedule, costs, and recommendations. Make sure your headings reflect this structure. Similarly, an activity report will need to detail the date and location of the activity, its purpose or goal, any contacts made as a result of the activity, and any recommendations the writer might have to offer. When determining which headings to use, think about the major logical components of your report and let those divisions define the structure.

organizing your report

As noted above, formal reports can be lengthy documents. Aside from the core introductory, discussion, and/or recommendation sections, there are often pages of supplemental material. This mix of documents enables the report to speak to a variety of audiences; some readers will read the report in its entirety, others only the summary, budget, or technical information. In planning your research and writing strategy, focus first on the body of your report and leave time near the end to compile the supplemental documents.

The supplements help the reader navigate the information contained in the body of the report. They provide a frame for the document and enable readers to enter and exit the report at various points. *Front matter* refers to all the supplemental material that precedes your report: title page, summary, table of contents, list of figures/illustrations, etc. *Back matter* includes the supplements that follow the body of the report: references, appendices, etc. Below are descriptions of some of the more writing-intensive supplements.

Transmittal document

This document is usually formatted as a memo (for an internal audience, such as your boss) or a business letter (for an external audience, such as a client). It is not bound with the report but rather is attached to it as a kind of cover letter announcing the report to the intended reader (usually, the person or people who commissioned it). Use it to introduce the report, highlight any key elements, offer suggestions for follow-up, and/ or acknowledge the contributions of others.

Summary

The Summary, sometimes called the Executive Summary or Abstract, boils the entire report down to its essential purpose, scope, findings, and conclusions. Unless your report is very long, try to keep this section to about 250 words. The information should appear in the same order it appears in the report, and should not include any data that does not appear in the report. Think of the summary as a kind of highlight-reel: it should provide readers with a snapshot of the entire discussion and enable them to grasp the gist of the report as a whole. The summary should thus be able to stand alone as a separate document, quite apart from the report itself. Write this section with particular care—sometimes it is the only part of the report your supervisor will actually read.

Appendices

An appendix usually contains material that is important to the report but difficult to integrate into the body of the text. Appendices often include interview transcripts, surveys, complex formulas, detailed technical information, statistics, or large, complex illustrations that take up multiple pages. All of this data is essential, but it can disrupt the unity or coherence of the body of the report. Including the information as an appendix allows the reader to access it as needed, rather than wade through it in the middle of the discussion. When compiling your materials, use a separate appendix for each major item and be sure to refer to the relevant appendix at appropriate points in your report: e.g., (see Appendix A).

putting it all together: a sample sequence

Transmittal Document	Title Page	Summary	Table of Contents
		ii	iii

Introduction	Discussion	Discussion	Discussion
1 ...			

Conclusions	Recommend-ations*	References	Appendix A
	10	11	12

*(May be combined with Conclusions as a single section)

some notes on email

In many cases, email has replaced short memos and phone calls as a means of quick and easy business communication, and for good reason. Email is fast, efficient, and leaves a footprint. If necessary, you can track a conversation simply by reviewing the back and forth of email messages. This is one thing that makes email so appealing and useful in a business environment—it helps you retrace your steps. It is also a reason to treat email with care. Although often exchanged by individuals, email is never private. Never include something in an email that you would not include in a more obviously public document.

Also, because email is such a common means of personal communication, it is easy to adopt an overly familiar tone in business or professional emails. Try to avoid this faux pas. Remember to address your recipient in a fashion that reflects your relationship with him or her. "Hey there" might be an appropriate greeting for a friend, but not so much for an email to your Economics professor asking for an extension—and even less so to your boss. And don't even think of forwarding the joke email that your old roommate sent you last week.

nine Writing in the Sciences

All academic disciplines have particular conventions and preferences when it comes to writing. These shared assumptions, formats, and styles of communicating are part of what creates *discourse communities*—the circles of conversation amongst students, professors, researchers, and colleagues that make up academic research and study. Sociologists have particular ways of discussing sociology, film majors of film, chemists of chemistry, bioethicists of bioethics. Each discipline has its own jargon—its own vocabulary—which serves as a kind of discipline-specific shorthand. Further, disciplines also have conventions for formatting and citing information. This, again, creates some logical shortcuts for readers, enabling them to get at information more efficiently.

The natural and applied sciences have a number of forms and conventions that distinguish their writing from that of the humanities or social sciences. Take, for example, the lab report. In the sciences, lab reports are the mother tongue of academic communication. If you wish to communicate effectively in a scientific context, learning the basic linguistics of lab reports is crucial.

IMRAD: formatting your lab report

IMRAD is an acronym that lays out the basic format of lab reporting: Introduction, Materials and Methods, Results, and Discussion. Although some lab report formats will add to or adapt these headings, the IMRAD format remains the essential template for discussing lab results. It presents a problem or question, explains the method used to explore that question (in enough detail that someone else could replicate your experiment), reports the results of the investigation, and finally considers the implications of those results in light of the initial question. The following chart provides a roadmap of the essential questions addressed in each section.

SECTION	PURPOSE	ANSWERS THESE QUESTIONS
Introduction	Explains central question Gives context for the investigation Cites any relevant literature Names chosen approach States primary results	What did you do? Why did you do it? Who else has done similar or related work? How did you do it? What happened?
Materials and Methods	Details the experimental procedure step by step	How could someone else replicate your experiment?
Results	Reports, in detail, the results of the investigation	What actually happened?
Discussion	Comments on the significance of the results Suggests refinements, applications Offers possibilities for further study	Did the experiment do what you expected it to? Why or why not? How might the experiment be improved or adapted? What next?

It is important to note that the discussion section does not merely restate the results section; it interprets the results. The discussion is your opportunity to evaluate your procedure, to emphasize its strengths or critique its weaknesses. It is also a chance for you to imagine where you might go next. What are the implications of your findings? How do they illuminate or contradict the results of other studies? What further applications might there be of your method, of your hypothesis? These are the kinds of questions your discussion section should consider.

abstracts: making the essentials concrete

Often, especially in the case of larger projects or reports prepared for publication, a lab report will also include an abstract. This section precedes the introduction and provides the reader with the essential gist of the overall project. A good abstract will be brief (100–200 words) and will answer the big what, how, and why questions of your project (What did you do? Why did you do it? How did you do it? What happened? Why are the results interesting?). This section is similar to an introduction in that it lays out the essential logic of your project; however, it differs in that it omits information about relevant literature and includes information from the discussion.

Although the abstract will be the first thing your reader reads, it should be the last thing you write. That way, you'll have the most comprehensive understanding of your report and will be more successful at boiling things down to their essentials. When drafting the abstract, start by pulling the key ideas out of each section. In short, dissect your report. Try to articulate the most important points of each section in a sentence or two and then work to shape those details into a single, succinct, and coherent paragraph. An abstract is not just a summary, however, so don't just cut and paste sentences from your report. Instead, think of it as a separate document that presents a snapshot of your work.

passive voice: it's not all about you

Another distinctive feature of scientific writing is the use of the passive voice (see Chapter Five). Remember, the difference between active and passive voice lies in the relationship between the subject of a sentence and its verb. If the subject is the agent of action (i.e., if the subject does the action of the verb), the construction is active; if the subject receives the action of the verb (i.e., if the subject has the action done to it), then the construction is passive.

The researcher diluted the samples with 100ml of H_2O.

This sentence is written in the active voice. The subject ("researcher") performs the action of the verb ("diluted") on the object ("samples"). However, in science writing, this same action is usually voiced in a passive construction:

The samples were diluted with 100ml of H_2O.

Here the subject ("samples") *receives* the action of the verb ("were diluted"). The subject does not perform the action but instead has the action performed upon it. The agent of the action (the researcher, presumably) is invisible, at least grammatically.

The reasons for this shift are simple. The fact that a researcher performed this action is understood by the reader, so there is no need to include that detail in the sentence. Furthermore, science writing needs to maintain an objective stance. It is intentionally impersonal. A good lab report will detail the experiment in such a way that anyone, in any lab, should be able to replicate the results, be they in Beijing or Barcelona. To this end, a lab report focuses on the experiment itself, not on the people who performed it. For this reason, avoid the first person in lab reports. A methods section would not state that "I gathered 50 samples"; rather it would simply state that "50 samples were gathered". The passive voice, in this case, sharpens the focus of the statement. The active voice would simply clutter the point with unnecessary, and self-evident, information. When reading your lab report, the reader needs to know what, how, and why things happened the way they did. Knowing who did what in the experiment is of no real concern—that is what the authorship credit is for.

giving credit: documentation formats

Unlike other disciplines, the sciences do not use a single, standardized documentation format. Documentation styles in science tend to be journal-specific: the editors of *Nature* prefer one format while those of the *British Journal of Cancer* prefer another. For this reason, it is important to be familiar with the most commonly used documentation formats, and to make sure you know which one your professor, or editor, prefers. Most science documentation is based on one of three general formats: the name-and-year system, the alphabet-number system, and the citation-order system.

The name-and-year system involves in-text references: the author's name and the publication date of a given source are listed in a parenthetical reference within the text of your document. For example, a 2015 article written by Semple and Messenger would be cited (Semple and Messenger, 2015). The reader would then look to the References section of the paper to find out the rest of the publication information. Note that, unlike similar formats in the social sciences, no page number is provided. Articles with three authors can be cited using all three names in the first citation (Semple, Messenger, and Clarke, 2014) and then be shortened using *et al.* in the remaining citations (Semple *et al.*, 2014). If an article has more than three authors, use the name of the lead author followed by *et al.* each time you cite it. In the References section, however, cite all of the authors named in the article.

The alphabet-number system numbers each reference in an alphabetical list. When referring to a reference in the text, simply include the number of the article in superscript, as one would a footnote or endnote, or in square brackets. For example, if the Semple, Messenger, and Clarke article were number 25 in your References list, then your sentence would adopt one of the following formats:

In emergency-room patients, however, cardio-pulmonary distress can often be attributed to waiting-room stress.[25]

In emergency-room patients, however, cardio-pulmonary distress can often be attributed to waiting-room stress [25].

Every reference to a given article is made using the same number. You may end up citing reference 25 a dozen times in your paper, while referring to reference 13 only once.

The citation-order system (often called IEEE documentation in Engineering) is a variation on this approach. Instead of being numbered alphabetically, citations are numbered in sequence. The first reference in the paper is number one; the second is number two, and so on. Again, the references are noted in either superscript or square brackets, as above. However, each reference is given only one number. If you refer to a source more than once, use the original number each time. That number will correspond to the listing on your References page.

Regardless of the format you choose, the References page will provide the full publication information for the source. That publication information should include the authors' names, date of publication, title, source (journal title and volume, for example), and page number. For example:

Semple I, Messenger D, Clarke JL (2014) False positives for the defibrillator: the effects of stress on cardio-pulmonary distress in emergency room patients. *Emergent Care* 201: 147–156.

When in doubt about proper formatting, check the documentation styles used in your source material.

Use their References pages as a guide for your own. Alternatively, if you have been asked to follow the format of a particular journal, go to that journal's web site. Most science journal web sites include a page of submission guidelines that outline their formatting requirements in detail.

tone: be direct and be objective

Generally speaking, when writing in the sciences, try to maintain a direct and concise style. Focus on concrete details. Use plain-spoken, direct language to undergird any jargon and discipline-specific vocabulary. Your content will be sophisticated enough; don't clutter your prose with either extravagant or imprecise expressions. If the resulting solution of your experiment is a pale blue, opaque liquid then describe it as such, not as the "hazy blue of a Toronto sky." Avoid all temptations to wax poetic. Ultimately, like the researcher in the lab report, effective science writing does not draw attention to itself. Instead, it focuses on the matter under investigation—the procedures, the results, the implications—and explores this information as precisely and objectively as possible. Focus on the content—what you did, how you did it, what you discovered—and allow the formats and conventions of your discipline to help you communicate your findings.

Confusable Words: Usage and Misusage

accept / except

Accept is a verb meaning receive. *Except* is usually a preposition or conjunction meaning "but for" or "other than"; when used as a verb it means "to leave out."

affect / effect

Affect is a verb meaning "to act upon or influence." *Effect* is most commonly used as a noun meaning "result" or "impact"; *effect* can also be used as a verb meaning "to bring about."

alot

While you may get away with writing *alot* in an informal letter, likely your word processor will not even allow you to type it as one word. *Alot* is not a standard English word, and even *a lot* is rather unbecoming in formal prose. The sound-alike word *allot* is a verb meaning "to assign or distribute a portion of something."

alright / all right

Perhaps because we tend to pronounce *all right* as though it were one word, the *alright* spelling has appeared. While the familiar words *altogether* and *already* were once two words, the spelling of *alright* for *all right* is still considered unacceptable by most dictionaries, though the single word spelling is widely used. You should not use *alright* in formal, academic writing.

amount / number

Use *amount* with a singular noun that names a quantity that you cannot count (confidence, food, work, gold). Use *number* with a plural noun that names a quantity that you can count (cars, shoes, accountants, children).

beside / besides

Beside is a preposition meaning "next to." *Besides* is a preposition meaning "except" or "in addition to," as well as an adverb meaning "in addition."

between / among

Use *between* when referring to two things ("between a rock and a hard place") and *among* when referring to more than two persons or things ("among the members of her class").

complement / compliment

Complement with an *e* refers to things that fit together and is related to the word *complete*; *compliment* with an *i* is something *I* give to someone who is deserving of praise.

continual / continuous

Continual means that something recurs constantly: "His dinner was continually interrupted by phone calls from telemarketers." *Continuous* means that something never stops: "The continuous re-booting of her computer was a sure sign of a virus."

could of / would of / should of

These phrases are actually misspellings of spoken contractions. They are written correctly as *could have*, *would have*, and *should have*. Never use "of" in these phrases, or the contraction forms ("could've," "would've," etc.), in print.

defuse / diffuse

A potential conflict or argument is *defused*, made less explosive, or rendered powerless: the word was originally used only by explosives experts. The sound-alike verb *diffuse* means "to spread something around."

delusion / illusion

A *delusion* is a pathological condition in which an individual believes something to be true that is categorically untrue. An *illusion* is a temporary false perception or misleading appearance. One can *suffer from delusions* (a form of mental affliction) but not from *illusions*.

different from / different than

In most cases, *different from* is the correct usage. Things differ *from* each other. However, in a comparison of many differing items, one item might be *more different than* the others, but in this case "than" is connected to the word "more" (as in "more than") not the word "different."

discreet / discrete

A *discreet* person is tactful, shows good judgement, or is able to keep a secret: "Before accepting the proposal, the millionaire made discreet inquiries into her fiancé's personal history." *Discrete* refers to something that is separate and distinct: "The resulting report was divided into three discrete sections: former marriages, bankruptcies, and criminal activity."

disinterested / uninterested

Disinterested means "impartial" or "having no bias." *Uninterested* means "bored."

eminent / imminent

An *eminent* person is someone of distinction. An *imminent* disaster is likely to occur at any moment.

---

etc.

Some usage commentators state that *etc.* should not be used in formal writing, that it is the sign of a lazy writer. Other usage commentators suggest that *etc.* be used only when a list could include several other items that are reasonably obvious, and that it should never be used in reference to people. If and when you use *etc.*—an abbreviation of the Latin phrase *et cetera*, meaning "and so forth"—it should always be accompanied by a period, regardless of where the word appears in the sentence.

everyday / every day

Everyday is an adjective meaning "ordinary." *Every day* is a two-word phrase (the adjective *every* modifies the noun *day*) meaning "daily" or "each day."

fewer / less

Fewer refers to a quantity that you can count (cars, shoes, accountants, children). *Less* refers to a quantity that you cannot count (confidence, food, work, gold).

flaunt / flout

Flaunt is a verb meaning "to show off" or "to display ostentatiously." *Flout* is a verb meaning "to disregard" or "to scorn."

hopefully

Consider the meaning of the following sentence: "Hopefully, Bidwell ran for city council." It could be that the writer means to imply that Bidwell was such a fine upstanding individual with evident leadership qualities that the writer hopes she ran for city council. Or perhaps the sentence makes a statement about Bidwell, who, with a hope for a purposeful and adventurous future, ran for city council. The problem with *hopefully* is that in form it is an adverb meaning "in a hopeful manner," yet since the early 1930s the word has been used to mean something like "let's hope," or "it is hoped that," as in the sentence, "Hopefully, the soccer game won't be rained out tonight." In conversation and in informal writing, *hopefully* is frequently used in this way. To avoid ambiguous statements such as the first sample sentence, in formal writing you should restrict the use of *hopefully* to contexts in which it means "in a hopeful manner," and use "I hope" or "it is hoped that" to express the more general "let's hope."

imply / infer

A speaker or writer *implies*, "hints at" or "suggests" an intended meaning; the listener or reader *infers* from what is said or written, and "comes to a reasoned conclusion or deduction."

---

in / into

In generally refers to a location within: "She sat in the car all day." *Into* refers to the action of going toward the location: "The cyclist ran into the car."

into (for "interested in")

If you are into using *into* to mean "interested in," get out of it. This is a 1960s colloquialism that does not belong in formal writing and should be dropped from casual speech as well. No dictionary or language expert is *into* this usage.

irregardless / regardless

Regardless means "without regard to" (the suffix *-less* conveys negation). *Irregardless* is a non-standard word that by its appearance would mean, illogically, "without without regard" (the prefix *ir-* conveys negation as well). The most widely used illiteracy in English, *irregardless* is likely a blend of *irrespective* and *regardless*. Do not use it.

is when / is where

Neither of these phrases is considered grammatical in English. Do not write something like "Absolute zero *is when* all the atoms in a molecule stop moving." Rather, rewrite the sentence by inserting a noun after *is*, or, if appropriate, by replacing *is* with *occurs* ("Absolute zero occurs when ..."). Better still, change the sentence altogether: "Absolute zero is the theoretical temperature at which all the atoms in a molecule stop moving."

its / it's

Like *yours* or *hers*, *its* is a possessive pronoun that indicates possession without an *'s*. It is often confused with *it's*, a contraction for "it is" or "it has." The apostrophe indicates the missing letter(s). There is no such word form as *its'*.

militate / mitigate

To *militate* against something means "to work or operate (usually) against it." To *mitigate* a circumstance means "to reduce its severity, make it less serious."

phenomenon / phenomena

Phenomena is the plural form of singular *phenomenon*. It is incorrect to use *phenomenas* or *phenomenons*. The clipped form *phenom* is sportswriter's slang.

principal / principle

As an adjective, *principal* means "first or most important." The most important person to a grade-schooler is the school *principal* (noun), who wants to be considered a *pal*. The homophone *principle* is a noun meaning "a rule of conduct or law." Principals are usually people of principle, we hope.

---

quote / quotation

Quote is a verb; *quotation* is a noun. In formal writing you should not use *quote* to mean *quotation*, though in speech this is more acceptable.

reason is because / reason why

In both of these commonly used phrases, one word is redundant. The word *because* means "for the reason that." So, when you use *the reason is because* you are saying, "the reason is for the reason that," most certainly an unnecessary repetition. The same goes for the equally popular *the reason why*, where *why* in context means "for that reason." Do not write, "The *reason* I did not submit my essay on time *is because* I had to take my housemate to the Emergency Room." Rather, make the sentence tidier and avoid the redundancy: "I did not submit my essay on time *because* I had to take my housemate to the Emergency Room."

systemic / systematic

Something that is *systemic*, like racism or discrimination, operates within a system and is hard to detect. A *systematic* approach to a task is carried out in a thorough, orderly way.

than / then

Than is used when making a comparison: *She is wiser than me; then* refers to time, indicating when or in what order an action or event occurred. Because these words sound alike, *than* is frequently misspelled as *then*.

unique (really, very, somewhat)

Unique is an absolute term meaning "one of a kind." Therefore it cannot sensibly be modified with words like *rather, really, very, somewhat, quite, most,* or *more.* How can a thingamajig be *very* one of a kind or the *most* one of a kind? If the thingamajig is one of a kind, it is unique. If, however, there are other thingamajigs like it—though few to be found—use words such as *rare, uncommon,* or *unusual* to describe it.

who / whom

Who is a pronoun that is used as the subject of a sentence or clause. *Whom* is the object form of the pronoun. A *who* can be sensibly replaced with *he* or *she*, a *whom* with *him* or *her*.

From the Publisher

A name never says it all, but the word "Broadview" expresses a
good deal of the philosophy behind our company. We are open to
a broad range of academic approaches and political viewpoints.
We pay attention to the broad impact book publishing and book
printing has in the wider world; we began using recycled stock
more than a decade ago, and for some years now we have used
100% recycled paper for most titles. Our publishing program is
internationally oriented and broad-ranging. Our individual titles
often appeal to a broad readership too; many are of interest as
much to general readers as to academics and students.

Founded in 1985, Broadview remains a fully independent
company owned by its shareholders—not an imprint
or subsidiary of a larger multinational.

For the most accurate information on our books (including
information on pricing, editions, and formats) please visit our
website at www.broadviewpress.com. Our print books and
ebooks are also available for sale on our site.

broadview press
www.broadviewpress.com

RECYCLED
Paper made from recycled material
FSC® C103567

FSC
www.fsc.org

The interior of this book is printed on 100% recycled paper.

PERMANENT   100%   BIO GAS   Ancient Forest Friendly™